Out of Exile

TED TORGERSEN

INK START MEDIA
265 Eastchester Dr Ste 133 #102
High Point NC 27262

Out of Exile

TED TORGERSEN

Table of Contents

CHAPTER ONE
Out of Exile

CHAPTER TWO
Patch Hell a Mile

CHAPTER THREE
Chenrezig

CHAPTER FOUR:
Mongoose Dentist

CHAPTER FIVE:
The Wind and the Goats

CHAPTER SIX
David Captain

CHAPTER SEVEN:
The Soap Mills of France

Fallen Empire
and Other Writings

Fallen Empire

Other Writings

The Four Directions

The Endless

Addendum

Author's Preface

This book, and the one that follows, represent my life's work. *Fallen Empire* was written after I completed *Out of Exile*, during a time when I explored possibilities for publication. By the time the opportunity to self publish presented itself, I found I had written another book which is included in this one volume.

As a youth I was inspired by song lyrics, and naively entrusted what I wrote to individuals who simply stole them. Not only did I receive nothing, but was actively persecuted which resulted in my being blacklisted, through no fault of my own, while at university.

During my education I was exposed to the poetry of Robert Burns, who is primarily known for the internal harmonics of his lyrics. I discovered that the use of rhyme, assonance and meter that comprise internal harmonics were present in the lyrics I had already written. I present most of the best of them here for literary purposes only, for although the songs have been sung, marketed and copy written long since, they are mine. The songs that I wrote after this time were given away, most notably those that appear in the 1970s movie *The Harder They Come*, starring Jimmy Cliff. Those were given gladly to my brethren in the West Indies, as payment in kind for the safe harbour I enjoyed there.

The rest of *Out of Exile* was written between 2006 and 2010, and represents my attempts to recapture the internal harmonics that at times flowed so freely in my youth. I also wrote poetry and one short nonfiction story, *Patch Hell a Mile*. Inspired by Robert Burns, I wrote in the vernacular of my day, and as my cultural orientation is twofold, both working class American English and the West Indian dialect as spoken in Tobago are used. The reader will notice that the use of pronouns differs from standard usage. "Me" usually replaces "I", "we" almost always replaces "us" and "our" and "he" and "she" invariably replace "him" and "her". Also, my spelling of certain words is at times creative. This makes it appear that I am two different people trying to sound alike but not succeeding.

I cannot thank the people who inspired and encouraged me enough, most notably Dr. Robert S. Kinsman of U.C.L.A. and Professor V. S. Naipaul of the University of the West Indies. I am also indebted to my daughter, Thea for technical assistance. And, finally, my sincere thanks for the guidance received at Lost Coast Press, without which this work would never have existed.

Respectfully submitted,

December 2014

CHAPTER ONE

Out of Exile

Ripple

If my words did glow,
with the gold of sunshine,
and my tunes were played
on the harp, unstrung,
would you hear my voice
come through the music,
would you hold it near,
as it were your own?
It's a hand me down,
the thoughts are broken,
perhaps they're better left unsung.
I don't know,
don't really care:
let there be songs
to fill the air.

(chorus)

Ripple, in still waters,
where there is no pebble tossed,
nor wind to blow.

Reach out your hand,
if your cup be empty.
If your cup is full,
may it be again.
Let it be known:
there is a fountain
that was not made
by the hands of men.
There is a road,
no simple highway,
between the dawn
and the dark of night.
And if you go,
no one may follow,
that path is for
your steps alone.

(chorus)

You can choose,
to lead must follow.
But if you fall,
you fall alone.
If you should stand,
then who's to guide you?
If I knew the way,
I would take you home...

———

Truckin'

Truckin', got my chips cashed in,
keep truckin', like the do dah man,
together, all the rest in line,
just keep truckin' on.

Here it's me, and I'm splashin'
my keys on main street,
Chicago, New York, Detroit,
and it's all the same street;
the typical city involved in the typical daydream,
hang it up and see what tomorrow brings.

Dallas, got a soft machine,
Houston, too close to New Orleans,
New York, got the ways and means,
and just won't let you be.
Most of the cats you meet on the street
speak of true love,
most of the time they're sittin' and cryin' at home.
One of these days they know they gotta get goin',
out of the door and down to the street all alone.

Truckin', like the do dah man,
once told me you gotta pay your can.
Some times the cards ain't worth a dime,
if you don't lay 'em down.

Some time the light's all shinin' on me,
other times I can barely see,
lately it occurs to me:
what a long strange trip it's been.

What in the world ever became of Sweet Jane?
She lost the struggle, you know she isn't the same.
Livin' on reds, vitamin C and cocaine,
all her friends can say is "ain't it a shame".

Truckin', up to Buffalo,
been thinkin', 'bout the mellow slow,
it takes time, to pick a place to go,
and just keep truckin' on.

Sittin' and starin' out of the hotel window,
goddamn, but they're gonna kick the door in again.
I like to get some sleep before I travel,
but if you got a warrant,
I guess you're gonna come in.

Busted, down on Bourbon Street,
set up, like a bowling pin,
knocked down, it gets to wearin' thin,
they just won't let you be.

You sick of hangin' around, you like to travel,
you tired of travelin', you want to settle down.
I guess they can't revoke us all the time,
get out of the door and have a look all around.

Some time the light's all shinin' on me,
other times I can barely see.
Lately it occurs to me:
what a long strange trip it's been.

Truckin', I'm a goin' home,
whoa, whoa, baby, back where I belong.
Back home, sit down and patch my bones,
and get back truckin' on.

———————

Uncle John's Band

Well, the first days are the hardest days,
don't you worry any more,
'cause when life looks like easy street,
there is danger at your door.
Think this through with me,
let me know your mind,
whoa, oh, what I want to know
is: are you kind?

It's a buck dancer's choice
my friends, better take my advice.
You know all the rules by now,
and the fire from the ice.
Will you come with me,
won't you come with me?
Whoa, oh, what I want to know:
will you come with me?
God damn, well I declare,
have you seen the like?
There was a guild of cannonballs,
their motto is "don't tread on me".

Come, hear Uncle John's Band,
playing to the tide.
Come with me or go alone,
he's come to take his children home.

It's the same story they told all we,
it's the only one we know.
Like the morning sun you come,
and like the wind you go.
Ain't no time to hate,

barely time to wait.
Whoa, oh, what I want to know, oh,
where does the time go?

I live in a silver mine,
and I call it Beggar's Tomb.
I got me a violin,
and I make it call the tune.
Anybody's choice,
I can hear your voice:
whoa, oh, what I want to know, oh,
how does the song go?
(chorus)

Come, hear Uncle John's Band,
by the riverside.
Got some things to talk about,
here beside the rising tide.
Come, hear Uncle John's Band,
playing to the tide.
Come along or go alone,
he's come to take his children home.

Whoa, oh, what I want to know, oh,
how does the song go?

(chorus)

———

Casey Jones

(chorus)

Drivin' that train, high on cocaine,
Casey Jones, you better watch your speed.
Trouble ahead, trouble behind,
and, you know, that notion just crossed my mind....

This old engine makes it on time,
leaves at the station 'bout a quarter to nine,
hits River Junction at seventeen to,
at a quarter to ten, you know, it's drivin' again.

(chorus)

Trouble ahead, the Lady in Red,
take my advice, you'd be better off dead.
Switchman sleepin', train hundred and two
is on the wrong track and headed for you.

(chorus)

Trouble with you, is the trouble with me,
got two good eyes, but you still don't see.
Come 'round the bend, you know it's the end,
the fireman screams and the engine just gleams.

(chorus)

(repeat chorus)

———————

One More Saturday Night

I went down to the mountain,
I was drinkin' some wine,
looked up in the Heaven,
Lord, and saw a mighty sign.
Written fire across the Heaven,
plain in black and white:
get prepared, there's gonna be a party, tonight.

(chorus)

Uh huh, hey Saturday night,
say, uh huh,
one more Saturday night.
Hey, Saturday night.

Everybody's dancin', down the local armory,
with a basement full of dynamite and live artillery.
Temperature keeps risin', everybody gettin' high,
come the rockin' stroke of midnight,
the place is gonna fly.

(chorus)

Turn on channel six,
the president comes on the news,
said, "I get no satisfaction,
that's why I sing the blues."
His wife said, "Don't get crazy,
Lord, you know just what to do,
crank up that old Victrola,
break out your rockin' shoes".

(chorus)

Then, God, way up in Heaven,
for whatever it was worth,
thought He'd have a big old party,
thought He'd call it Planet Earth.
Don't worry about tomorrow,
you'll know it when it comes,
when the rock and roll music
meets the risin' planet sun.

(chorus)

Hey, there, Saturday night,
hey, there Saturday night.
There's nothin' you can't fight,
hey, there Saturday night,
one more Saturday,
one more Saturday night.

Hey, there, Saturday night,
hey, there Saturday night.
Hey, there Saturday night,
one more Saturday,
one more Saturday night.

(repeat)

———————————

Franklin's Tower

In another time's forgotten space,
two eyes looked from your mother's face.
Wildflower seed on the sand and stone,
may the four winds blow you safely home.

(chorus)

Roll away the dew,
roll away the dew,
roll away the dew,
roll away the dew.

I tell you where the four winds dwell,
in Franklin's Tower there hangs a bell.
It can ring tonight, today,
ring like fire when you lose your way.

(chorus)

God save the child who's raised that way.
They have one good thing there, and you can tell.
One watched by night,
one watched by day.
If you get confused,
listen to the music play.

Some come to laugh, and pass the way,
some come to make just one more day.
Whichever way your pleasure tends,
if you plant ice, you gonna harvest wind.

(chorus)

Franklin's Tower, where the four winds sleep,
like fourteen hounds, and the lightening speaks.
Wildflower seed in the sand again,
may the four winds blow you home, again.

(chorus)

———————————

Touch of Grey

Must be getting early,
clocks are running late.
All lit up, the morning sky
looks so phony.
Dawn is breaking everywhere,
light a candle, curse the glare,
draw the curtains, I don't care,
'cause it's alright.

I will get by,
I will get by,
I will get by,
I will survive.

I see you got your fists out,
say your piece, and get out.
I guess I get the gist of it,
but it's alright.
Sorry that you feel that way,
the only thing I've got to say
is every silver lining has a touch of grey.

I will get by,
I will get by,
I will get by,
I will survive.

It's a lesson to me,
the evils, and the Pagans,
and the sea.
The abc's
we all must face,
to try and keep a little grace.

It's a lesson to me,
the delta's in the East, in the breeze.
The abc's
we all think of,
to try to get a little love.
I know the rent is in arrears,
the dog has not been fed in years,
it's even worse than it appears,
but it's alright.

Now I give them kerosene,
she can't read at seventeen,
the words she knows are all obscene,
but it's alright.
I will get by,
I will get by,
I will get by,
I will survive.

Sugar's on the hands and fists,
there's nothing much to it,
whistle through your teeth and spit,
and it's alright.
Oh well, a touch of grey
kind of suits you, anyway.
That is all I have to say,
and it's alright.

I will get by,
I will get by,
I will get by,
I will survive.

We will get by,
we will get by,
we will get by,
we will survive.

———————

Sugar Magnolia

Sugar Magnolia, blossoms blooming,
heads all empty, and I don't care.
Saw my baby down by the river,
knew she had to come up, soon, for air.
Sweet Blossom, come on, under the willow.
We can have high times, if you'll abide.
We can discover the wonders of nature,
rollin' in the rushes, down by the riverside.

She's got everything delightful,
she's got everything I need,
takes the wheel when I'm seein' double,
pays my ticket, when I speed.

She comes skimmin' through rays of violet,
she can wade in a drop of dew,
she don't come, and I don't follow,
waits back stage while I sing to you.

Well, she can dance a Cajun rhythm,
jump like a Willys in four wheel drive.
She's a summer love in the spring, fall and winter,
she can make happy any man alive.

Sugar Magnolia, ringin' that bluebell.
Caught up in sunlight, come out singin',
I'll walk you in sunshine,
come on, honey, come along with me.

She's got everything delightful,
she's got everything I need,
a breeze in the pines in the sun and bright moonlight,
crazy in the sunlight, yes indeed.

Sometime, when the cuckoo's cryin',
when the moon is halfway to town,
sometimes when the night is dyin',
I take me out and I wander 'round.
I wander 'round.
Sunshine daydream, walkin' in the tall trees,
goin' where the wind goes,
bloomin' like a red rose, even more pretty.
While I'm singin', I'm walkin' in the morning sunshine,
sunshine daydream, sunshine daydream,
walkin' in the sunshine.

Eyes of the World

Right outside this lazy summer home,
you ain't got time to call your soul a critic, no.
Right outside the lazy gate of winter's summer home,
I'm wondering where the nut-hatch winters.
Wings a mile long just carried that bird away.

(chorus)

Wake up to find out that you are the eyes of the world.
Your heart has its features, its homeland,
and thoughts of its own.
Right now, discover that you are the song
that the morning brings.
The heart has its seasons,
its evenings and songs of its own.

There comes a redeemer,
and he, slowly, too, fades away.
And there follows, his wagon behind him,
that's loaded with clay.
And the seeds that were silent,
all burst into bloom, and decay,
and the night comes so quiet,
it's close on the heels of the day.

(chorus)

Sometimes we live in no
particular way, but our own.
Sometimes, we visit your country
and live in your home.
Sometimes we ride on your horses,
sometimes, we walk alone,
sometimes the songs that we hear
are just songs of our own.

(chorus)

———————

Box of Rain

Look out of any window,
any morning,
any evening,
any day.
Maybe the sun is shinin',
birds are wingin',
no rain is fallin'
from a heavy sky.

(chorus)

What do you want me to do,
to do for you,
to see you through?
For this is all a dream we dreamed
one afternoon, long ago.

Walk out of any doorway,
feel your way,
feel your way
back, the day before.
Maybe you'll find direction,
around some corner
where it's still waitin' to meet you.

What do you want me to do,
to watch for you,
while you're sleepin'?
Then, please don't be surprised
when you find me dreamin', too.

Look into any eye,
if you find value,
you can see into another day.
Maybe it's been seen before,
through other eyes,
on other days,
while goin' home.

(chorus)

Walk into splintered sunrise,
inch your way through
dead dreams to another land.
Maybe you're tired and broken,
your tongue is twisted with words
half spoken and thoughts unclear.

What do you want me to do,
to do for you,
to see you through?

A box of rain will ease the pain,
and love will see you through.
Just a box of rain, wind and water:
believe it if you need it,
if you don't, just pass it on.

Sun and shadow, wind and rain,
in and out the window
like a moth before a flame.

And it's just a box of rain,
I don't know who put it there.
Believe it if you need it,
or leave it if you dare.

And it's just a box of rain,
or a ribbon for your hair.
Such a long, long time to be gone,
and a short time to be there.

———————

Ted Torgersen

U. S. Blues

Red and white,
blue suede shoes,
I'm Uncle Sam,
how do you do?
Give me five,
I'm still alive.
Ain't no luck,
I learned to duck.

Check my pulse,
it don't change.
Stays seventy two
come shine or rain.
Wave the flag,
pop the bag,
rock the boat,
skin the goat.

(chorus)

Wave that flag,
wave it wide:
summer time has
come and gone,
my oh my.

I'm Uncle Sam,
that's who I am.
Been hidin' out
in a rock and roll band.
Shake the hand,
that shook the hand,
of P. T. Barnum
and Charlie Chan.

Shine your shoes,
light the fuse,
can you use
them old U. S. Blues?
I'll drink your health,
share your wealth,
run your life,
steal your wife.

(chorus)

Back to back,
chicken shack,
son of a gun,
better change your act.
We're all confused,
what's to lose?
You can call this song
the United States Blues.

(chorus)

My oh my oh my,
summer time has
come and gone,
my oh my.

———

The Music Never Stopped

There's mosquitoes on the river,
fish are rising up like birds.
It's been hot for seven weeks, now,
too hot to even speak, now.
Did you hear what I just heard?

Say, it might have been a fiddle,
or it could have been the wind.
But there seems to be a beat, now,
I can feel it in my feet, now.
Listen, here it comes again.

There's a band out on the highway,
they're high steppin' into town.
It's a rainbow full of sound,
it's fireworks, calliopes and clowns.
And everybody's dancin'.

Come on children, come on children,
come on, clap your hands.

Sun went down in honey,
moon came up in white,
you know the stars were spinnin' dizzy,
Lord, the band kept us so busy,
we forgot about the time.

There are bands beyond description,
like Jehovah's favorite choir,
people joinin' hand in hand,
while the music plays the band.
Lord, they're settin' up on fire.

Crazy rooster crowin' midnight,
balls of lightening roll along,
old men sing about their dreams,
women laugh and children scream,
and the band keeps playin' on.

Keep on dancin' through the daylight,
greet the morning air with song.
No one's noticed but the band's
all packed and gone.
Was it ever here at all?
But they kept on dancin'.

Come on, children, come on children,
come on clap your hands.

Well, the cool breeze came on Tuesday,
and the corn's a bumper crop.
And the fields are full of dancin',
full of singin' and romancin',
the music never stopped.

———————————

Castles Burning

Old man lying
by the side of the road,
with the lorries rolling by.
Blue moon sinking
from the weight of the load,
and the buildings scrape the sky.
Cold wind ripping
down the alley at dawn,
and the morning paper flies.
Dead man lying
by the side of the road
with the daylight in his eyes.

(chorus)

Don't let it bring you down,
it's only castles burning.
Find someone who's turning,
and you will come around.

Blind man running
through the light of the night,
with an answer in his hand;
come on down to the river of sight,
and you can really understand.
Red lights flashing
through the window in the rain:
can you hear the sirens moan?
White cane lying
in a gutter in the lane,
if you're walking home alone.

(chorus)

———————

Ted Torgersen

After the Gold Rush

Well, I dreamed I saw the knights in armor
comin', saying something about a queen.
There were peasants singing
and drummers drumming,
and the archer split the tree.
There was a fanfare blowin' to the sun
that was floating on the breeze:
look at mother nature on the run,
in the nineteen seventies.
Look at mother nature on the run,
in the nineteen seventies.

I was lyin' in a burned out basement,
with the full moon in my eyes.
I was hopin' for replacement,
when the sun burst through the skies.
There was a band playin' in my head,
and I felt like getting high.
I was thinkin' about what a friend had said,
I was hopin' it was a lie.
Thinkin' about what a friend had said,
I was hopin' it was a lie.

Well, I dreamed I saw the silver spaceships
lyin', in the yellow haze of the sun.
There were children cryin', and colors flyin'
all around the chosen ones.
All in a dream, all in a dream,
the loading had begun.
Flyin' mother nature's silver seed
to a new home in the sun.
Flyin' mother nature's silver seed
to a new home...

———

Sitting in Limbo

Sitting here in limbo,
but I know it won't be long.
Sitting here in limbo,
like a bird without a song.
Well, they're putting up positions,
but I know that my faith
will lead me on.

Sitting here in limbo,
waiting for the dice to roll.
Sitting here in limbo,
got some time to search my soul.

Well, they're putting up positions,
but I know that my faith
will lead me on.

I don't know where life will lead me,
but I know where I've been.
I can't say what life will show me,
but I know what I've seen.
Tried my hand at love and friendship,
all of that is past and gone.
This little boy is moving on.

Sitting here in limbo,
waiting for the tide to flow.
Sitting here in limbo,
knowing that I have to go.

Well, they're putting up resistance,
but I know that my faith
will lead me on.

I can't say what life will show me,
but I know what I've seen.
I can't say where life will lead me,
but I know where I've been.
Tried my hand at love and friendship,
all of that is past and gone.
This little boy is moving on.

Sitting here in limbo,
waiting for the tide to flow.
Sitting here in limbo,
knowing that I have to go.
Well, they're putting up resistance,
but I know that my faith
will lead me on.

———

Many Rivers to Cross

Many rivers to cross,
but I can't seem to find
my way over.
Wandering, I am lost,
as I travel along
the white cliffs of Dover.

Many rivers to cross,
and it's only my will
that keeps me alive.
I've been licked,
washed up for years,
and I merely survived,
because of my pride.

And this loneliness won't leave me alone,
it's such a drag to be on your own,
my woman left and she didn't say why,
well, I guess I have to try.

Many rivers to cross,
but just where to begin,
I'm playing for time.
There'll be times I find myself,
thinking of committing
some dreadful crime.

Yes, I've got many rivers to cross,
but I can't seem to find
my way over.
Wandering, I am lost,
as I travel along
the white cliffs of Dover.

Yes, I've got many rivers to cross,
and I merely survived,
because of my pride.

———————

The Harder They Come

Well, they tell me of a pie up in the sky,
waiting for me when I die,
but between the day you born and when you die,
they never seem to hear even your cry.

(chorus)

So, as sure as the sun will shine,
I'm gonna get my share, now, what's mine,
and then the harder they come,
the harder they fall, one and all.
The harder they come,
the harder they fall, one and all.

Well, the oppressors are trying to keep me down,
trying to drive me underground,
and they think that they have got the battle won,
I say, "Forgive them, Lord,
they know not what they've done."

(chorus)

And I keep on fighting for the things I want,
though I know that when you're dead you're gone.
But I'd rather be a free man in my grave,
than living as a puppet or a slave.

(chorus)

(repeat chorus)

Ted Torgersen

Ordinary Town

Common Cool, he was a proud young fool,
in a kick ass Walmart tie.
Up and down the main drag,
trippin' on the headlights rollin' by.
In the early dawn,
when the cars are gone,
does he hear the Master's call?
In the five and dime,
did he wake and find
he was only dreamin', after all?

'Cause this is an ordinary town,
and The Prophet stands apart.
This is an ordinary town,
and we brook no wayward heart.
Every highway leads
a prodigal back home,
to the ordinary sidewalks
you were born to roam.

Rock of Ages,
love contagious,
shine the Serpent Fire;
so sang the sage
of sixteen summers,
in the upstairs choir.
So sang the old dog
down the street,
beside his Wailing Wall.
"Go home, go home!"
the mayor cried,
when Jesus came to city hall.

'Cause this is an ordinary town,
and The Prophet stands alone.
This is an ordinary town,
and we crucify our own.
Every highway leads
a prodigal, again,
to the ordinary houses
you were brought up in.

Raised on hunches and junk food lunches,
and punch drunk ballroom steps,
you get to believin' you're even-steven
with the kids at Fast Track Prep.
So you dump your bucks
on a velvet tux,
and you run and join the dance.
But your holy shows,
and the Romans know,
you're just a child of circumstance.

'Cause this is an ordinary town,
and The Prophet has no face,
it is an ordinary town,
and the seasons run in place.
Every highway leads
a prodigal, in true,
to the ordinary angels
watchin' over you.

————

Hotel California

On a dark desert highway,
cool wind in my hair,
warm smell of colitas,
rising up through the air,
up ahead, in the distance,
I saw a shimmering light,
my head grew heavy
and my sight grew dim,
I had to stop for the night.
There she stood, in the doorway,
I heard the Mission bell,
I was thinking to myself,
this could be Heaven,
or this could be Hell.
Then she lit up a candle,
and she showed me the way,
there were voices down the corridor,
I thought I heard them say:

"Welcome to the Hotel California,
such a lovely place,
such a lovely place,
such a lovely place.
Plenty of room at the Hotel California,
any time of year,
you can find it here."

Her name is Tiffany Twisted,
she's got a Mercedes Benz.
She's got a lot of pretty, pretty boys
she calls friends.
How they danced in the courtyard,
sweet summer sweat,
some dance to remember,

some dance to forget.
So I called up the Captain,
please bring me my wine,
he said, "We haven't had that spirit
here since nineteen sixty nine."

And still those voices
are calling from far away,
wake you up in the middle of the night
just to hear them say:
"Welcome to the Hotel California,"
such a lovely place,
such a lovely place,
such a lovely place.
Livin' it up at the Hotel California,
what a nice surprise,
when you're alibied.

Mirrors on the ceiling,
pink champagne on ice,
she said, "We're all just prisoners here,
of our own device."
In the Master's chambers,
they're gathered for the feast,
they stab it with their steely knives,
but they just can't kill the beast.
The last thing I remember,
I was running for the door,
I had to find the passage back
to the place I was before.
"Relax", said the night man,
"we are programmed to receive,
you can check out any time you like,
but you can never leave."

Peaceful Easy Feeling

I like the way your sparking earrings lay,
against your skin, so brown,
and I want to sleep with you
in the desert, tonight,
with a billion stars all around.

(chorus)

'Cause I got a peaceful, easy feeling,
and I know you won't let me down,
'cause I'm already standing
on the ground.

And I found out a long time ago,
what a woman can do to your soul.
Aw, but she can't take you any way
you don't already know how to go.

(chorus)

I get this feelin' I may know you,
as a lover and a friend.
This voice keeps whispering,
in my other ear,
tells me I may never see you again.

(chorus)

Dire Wolf

In timbers up in 'Derrio
the wolves were runnin' 'round.
The winter was so hard and cold,
it froze ten feet 'neath the ground.

(chorus)

Don't murder me.
I beg of you,
don't murder me.
Please, don't murder me.

I sat down to my supper,
'twas a pot of redfish tea.
I said my prayers,
and went to bed,
that's the last they saw of me.

(chorus)

When I awoke, the Diet Wolf,
six hundred pounds of sin,
was grinning at my window,
all I said was "Come on in."

(chorus)

The Wolf came in,
I got my cards,
and sat down for a game.
I cut my deck to the Queen of Spades,
but the cards were all the same.

(chorus)

In the Back Walsh up in 'Derrio,
a black and bloody mine,
the Diet Wolf collects his due,
while the boys sing 'round the fire.

(chorus)

(repeat chorus)

_____

Ramble On, Rose

Just like Jack the Ripper,
just like Mojo Hand,
just like Billy Sunday,
in a shotgun, ragtime band.

Just like New York City,
just like Jericho,
paint the halls,
and climb the walls,
and get out, when they blow.

(chorus)

Did you say your name
was Ramblin' Rose?
Ramble on, baby,
settle down easy,
ramble on, Rose.

Just like Jack and Jill,
Mama told the sailor,
one heat up,
and one cool down,
see, nothin's for the tailor.

Just like Jack and Jill,
Pappa told the gaoler,
one go up,
and one go down,
do yourself a favor.

(chorus)

(refrain)

I'm gonna sing you
a hundred verses in ragtime.
I know this song,
it ain't never gone end.
I'm gonna march up and down
the long gone county line,
take you to the leader
of our band.

Just like Crazy Otto,
just like Wolfman Jack,
sittin' plush with a royal flush,
aces back to back.

Just like Mary Shelly,
just like Frankenstein,
break your chains,
and count your change,
and try to walk the line.

(chorus)

(refrain)

Goodbye, Mama and Pappa,
goodbye Jack and Jill,
the grass ain't greener,
the wine ain't sweeter,
either side of the hill.

(chorus)

———————

The Parrot

One time I was a dirt eating parrot,
'cause that's what I needed to be.
If you think, say, there is a reason,
you just ain't been talkin' to me.

Why are there no easy answers,
that remind us of what we forgot?
Sometimes something's like something,
but that's exactly what it is not.

How have I helped you this morning?
What's left for this afternoon?
They tell me something is coming,
but I hope it ain't anytime soon.

All this is just on the surface,
I gotta start digging, just now.
Sometimes I think I know what for,
but no one has ever said how.

So, I'm just a dirt eating parrot,
it's what I was meant to be.
Flyin's just work, it wasn't, at first,
but this time I needed to see.

———————————

Where Are You Been Gone

(chorus)

V. J. Naipaul,* where are you been gone,
where are you been gone?
Where are you been gone,
where are you been gone?

The nation all over looking for you,
and up to now nobody have a clue.
We search the forest and we search the town,
up to this day you still cannot be found.

We know you couldn't disappear just so,
this country is too small, where could you go?
Your family say that you gone too long,
they ask me to find you back with this song.

(chorus)

We pray to God, yes, for your safe return,
we ask of you to whom it may concern.
God never give you more than you can bear,
I know someone is hearing me out there.

The nights and days are slowly passing by,
the angels of forgiveness flying high,
I hear the sounds of traffic in the sky,
for those victims who suffered and died.

(chorus)

* With sincere apologies to V. S. Naipaul.
We pray so the Father knows your heart,
but you was kind and gentle from the start.
To those who have transgressed, for what it's worth,
I hope we still could find peace here on earth.

A nation in mourning, yes, every day,
a paradise no longer, we could say.
The forces of terrestrial now at hand,
the wrath of destruction engulf our land.

(chorus)

Ring Them Bells

Ring them bells, ye heathen,
from the city that dreams.
Ring them from the sanctuary,
'cross the valleys and streams,
for they deep, and they wide,
and the world's on its side,
and time is runnin' backwards,
and so is the bride.

Ring them bells, Saint Peter,
where the four winds blow.
Ring them with an iron hand,
so the people will know.
For it's rush hour now,
on the wheel and the plow,
and the sun is a goin' down
upon the sacred cow.

Ring them bells, Sweet Martha,
for the poor man's son.
Ring them bells so the world
will know that God is one.
For the shepherd is asleep,
where the widow weeps,
and the mountains are
filled with lost sheep.

Ring them bells
for the blind and the deaf.
Ring them bells
for those of us who are left.
Ring them bells
for the chosen few,
who will judge the many
when the game is through.
Ring them bells,
for the times of life,
for the child of Christ,
when innocence died.

Ring them bells, Saint Katherine's,
from the top of the room.
Ring them from the fortress
for the lilies that bloom.
For the lines are long,
and the fighting is strong,
and they breakin' down the difference
between right and wrong.

Handle with Care

Beef it up, and bat it around,
been sent up, and I been shut down,
you're the best thing I've ever found,
handle me with care.

Reputation's changeable,
situation's tolerable,
but baby, you're adorable,
handle me with care.

(chorus)

I'm so tired of bein' lonely,
I still have some love to give.
Won't you show me that you really care?
Everybody's got some body to lean on.
Put your body next to mine, and dream on.

I've been fogged up and I've been fooled,
I've been robbed and ridiculed.
Vacant senses and night school,
handle me with care.

Been stickin' up and terrorized,
sets of meaning, hypnotized,
overexposed, commercialized,
handle me with care.

(chorus)

I been uptight, and made a mess,
but I'll clean it up myself, I guess.
Oh, the sweet smell of success,
handle me with care.

Last Night

She was there at the bar,
she heard my guitar.
She was long and tall,
she was the queen of them all.

(chorus)
Last night,
thinkin' 'bout last night.
Last night,
thinkin' 'bout last night.

She was dark and discreet,
she was light on her feet.
We went up to her room,
and she lowered the boom.

(chorus)

Down below, they danced,
and sang in the street,
while up above, the walls
were steaming with heat.

(chorus)

I was feelin' no pain,
feelin' good in my brain.
I looked in her eyes,
they were full of surprise.

(chorus)

I asked her to marry me,
she smiled, and pulled out a knife.
She parted the beginning,
she said, "Your money or your life."

(chorus)

Now, I'm back at the bar,
she went a little too far.
She done me wrong,
all I got is this song.

(chorus)

———

End of the Line

Well, it's all right,
ridin' around in the breeze,
well, it's all right,
if you live the life you please.
Well, it's all right,
doin' the best you can,
well, it's all right,
as long as you lend a hand.

You can sit around,
and wait for the phone to ring,
at the end of the line,
waiting for someone to tell you everything,
the end of the line,
sit around and wonder what tomorrow brings,
the end of the line,
maybe a diamond ring.

Well, it's all right,
even if it's to say you're wrong,
well, it's all right,
sometimes you gotta be strong.
Well, it's all right,
as long as you got someone to lay,
well, it's all right,
every day is Christmas day.

Maybe somewhere down the road a ways,
at the end of the line,
you'll think of me and wonder
where I am, these days,
at the end of the line,
maybe down the road somewhere,
when somebody plays,
at the end of the line,
Purple Haze.

Well, it's all right,
even when push comes to shove,
well, it's all right ,
if you've got someone to love.
Well, it's all right,
everything will work out fine,
well, it's all right,
we're goin' to the end of the line.

Don't have to be ashamed of the car I drive,
at the end of the line,
I'm glad to be here, happy to be alive,
at the end of the line,
it don't matter if you're by my side,
the end of the line,
I'm satisfied.

Well, it's all right,
even if you're old and gray.
Well, it's all right,
you still got somethin' to say.
Well, it's all right,
remember to live and let live.
Well, it's all right,
the best you can do is to give.

Well, it's all right,
ridin' around in the breeze,
well, it's all right,
if you live the life you please.
Well, it's all right,
even if the sun don't shine,
well, it's all right,
we're goin' to the end of the line.

Diamonds on the Soles
of Her Shoes

She's a rich girl,
she don't try to hide it,
diamonds on the soles of her shoes.
He's a poor boy,
empty as a pocket,
empty as a pocket,
with nothin' to lose.
Sing: Ta Na Na, Ta Na Na Na,
she got diamonds on the soles of her shoes.
Ta Na Na, Ta Na Na Na,   .
she got diamonds on the soles of her shoes,
diamonds on the soles of her shoes,
diamonds on the soles of her shoes,
diamonds on the soles of her shoes,
diamonds on the soles of her shoes.

People say she's crazy,
she got diamonds on the soles of her shoes.
Well, that's one way to lose
these walking blues,
diamonds on the soles of your shoes.

She was physically forgotten,
and then she slipped into my pocket
with my car keys.
She said, "You've taken me for granted
because I please you,
wearing these diamonds."

And I could say: Oooh Oooh Oooh, Oooh,
as if everybody knows what I'm talking about,
as if everybody here would know,
exactly what I was talking about.
Talkin' about diamonds on the soles of her shoes.

She makes the sign of a teaspoon,
he makes the sign of a wave.
The poor boy changes clothes,
and puts on aftershave,
to compensate for his ordinary shoes.
And she said, "Honey, take me dancing,"
but they ended up by sleeping in a doorway
of a bodega's, and the lights all over Broadway,
wearing diamonds on the soles of their shoes.

And I could say: Oooh Oooh Oooh, Oooh,
and everybody here would know
what I was talking about,
I mean, everybody here would know
exactly what I was talking about.
Talking about diamonds....

People say I'm crazy,
I got diamonds on the soles of my shoes, yeah.
Well, that's one way to lose these walking blues,
diamonds on the soles of our shoes.

Ta Na Na, Ta Na Na Na

(repeat)

———————————

You Can Call Me Al

A man walks down the street,
he says, "Why am I soft in the middle, now?
Why am I soft in the middle,
the rest of my life is so hard.
I need a photo opportunity,
I want a shot at redemption,
don't wanna end up a cartoon,
in a cartoon graveyard."
Bone digger, bone digger,
dogs in the moonlight,
far away, my well lit door;
Mr. Beer Belly, Beer Belly,
get these mutts away from me, you know,
I don't find this stuff amusing any more.

(chorus)
If you'll be my bodyguard,
I can be your long lost pal.
I can call you Betty,
and, Betty, when you call me,
you can call me Al.

A man walks down the street,
he says, "Why am I short of attention?
Got a short little span of attention,
oh, my nights are so long.
Where's my wife and family?
What if I die here?
Who'll be my role model,
now that my role model is gone, gone?"

He ducked back down the alley
with some roly-poly little bat faced girl.
All along, along, there were incidents and accidents,
there were hints and allegations.

(chorus)

Man walks down the street,
it's a street in a strange world,
maybe it's the Third World,
maybe it's his first time around.
Doesn't speak the language,
he holds no currency, he is a foreign man.
He is surrounded by the sound, sound
of cattle in the marketplace,
scatterings and orphanages.
He looks around, around,
he sees angels in the architecture,
spinning in infinity.

(chorus)

If you'll be my bodyguard,
I can call you Betty.
If you'll be my bodyguard.
I can call you Betty.

———————————

Ted Torgersen

Slip Slidin' Away

(chorus)

Slip sliding away,
slip sliding away,
you know, the nearer your destination,
the more you're slip sliding away.

I know a man,
he came from my home town,
he wore his passion for his woman
like a thorny crown.
He said, "Dolores, I live in fear.
My love for you is so overpowering,
I'm afraid that I will disappear."

(chorus)
And I know a woman,
became a wife.
These are the very words she uses
to describe her life:
she said, "A good day,
ain't got no rain."
She said, "A bad day is when
I lie in bed and think of things
that mattered then."
(chorus)

And I know a father, who had a son,
he longed to tell him all the reasons
for the things he'd done.
He came a long way, just to explain.
He kissed his boy as he lay sleeping,
then he turned around and headed home again.

He's slip slidin'.
Slip sliding away,
you know, the nearer your destination,
the more you're slip sliding away.

And God only knows,
and God makes his plan.
The information's unavailable
to the mortal man.
We're workin' our jobs, collect our pay,
believe we're gliding down the highway,
when in fact we're slip sliding away.

(chorus)

(repeat chorus)

———————————

Late in the Evening

First thing I remember, I was lying in my bed,
it couldn't have been no more than one or two.
And I remember there was a radio,
comin' from the room next door,
and my mother laughed the way some ladies do.
Well, it's late in the evening,
and the music seeping through.

Next thing I remember, I am walkin' down the street,
I'm feelin' alright, I'm with my boys,
I'm with my troops, yeah.
And down along the avenue,
some guys were shootin' pool,
and I heard the sound of a capella groups, yeah.
Singin' late in the evening,
and all the girls out on the stoops, yeah.

Then I learned to play some lead guitar,
I was under age in this funky bar,
and I stepped outside to smoke myself a jay.
And when I come back to the room,
everybody just seemed to move,
and I turned my amp up loud and I began to play.
And it was late in the evening,
and I blew that room away.

First thing I remember, when you came into my life,
I said, "I'm gonna get that girl, no matter what I do."
Well, I guess I've been in love, before,
once or twice I been on the floor,
but I never loved no one the way that I love you.

And it was late in the evening,
and all the music seeping through.
The Obvious Child

Well, I'm accustomed to a smooth ride,
or maybe I'm a dog who's lost his bite.
I don't expect to be treated like a fool no more,
I don't expect to sleep through the night.
Some people say a lie's a lie's a lie,
but I say, "Why, why deny the obvious, child,
why deny the obvious, child?"

And in remembering a road side,
I am remembering a girl, when I was young.
And we said, "These songs are true,
these days are ours, these tears are free.
And hey, the cross is in the ballpark,
the cross is in the ballpark."

Had a lot of fun, had a lot of money.
We had a little son,
we thought we'd call him Sonny.
Sonny gets married and moves away,
Sonny has a baby and bills to pay,
Sonny gets sunnier day by day, by day, by day.

Well, I been wakin' up at sunrise,
I been following the light across my room.
I watch the night recede the room of my day.
Some people say the sky is just the sky,
but I say, "Why deny the obvious, child,
why deny the obvious, child?"

Sonny sits by his window and thinks to himself,
how it's strange that some rooms are like cages.
Sonny's yearbook from high school
is down from the shelf,
and he idly thumbs through the pages.
Some have died, some have fled from themselves,
or struggled from here to get there.
Sonny wanders beyond his interior walls,
runs his hands through his thinning brown hair.

Well, I'm accustomed to a smooth ride,
or maybe I'm a dog that's lost his bite.
I don't expect to be treated like a fool no more,
I don't expect to sleep the night.
Some people say a lie is just a lie,
but I say, "The cross is in the ballpark.
Why deny the obvious, child?"

Me and Julio Down By the Schoolyard

Mama Pajama rolled out of bed,
and she ran to the police station.
When your Papa found out,
he began to shout,
and he started the investigation.
It's against the law, it was against the law.
What your Mama saw, it was against the law.

Mama looked down, and spit on the ground,
every time my name gets mentioned.
Papa said, "Oh, if I get that boy,
I'm gonna stick him in the house of detention."

Well, I'm on my way,
I don't know where I'm goin'.
I'm on my way, I'm takin' my time,
but I don't know where.
Goodbye, Rosie, the Queen of Corona.
See me and Julio, down by the schoolyard.
See me and Julio, down by the schoolyard.

In a couple a days they come to take me away,
but the press let the story leak.
And when the radical priest come to get me released,
we was all on the cover of Newsweek.

And I'm on my way,
I don't know where I'm goin'.
I'm on my way, I'm takin' my time,
but I don't know where.
Goodbye, Rosie, the Queen of Corona.
See me and Julio, down by the schoolyard.
See me and Julio, down by the schoolyard.
See me and Julio, down by the schoolyard.

———————————————

All Around the World, or the Myth of Fingerprints

Over the mountain, down in the valley,
lives a former talk show host,
everybody knows his name.
He said, "There's no doubt about it,
it was the myth of fingerprints,
I've seen them all, and man,
they're all the same."

Well, the sun gets weary,
and the sun goes down,
ever since the watermelon.
And the lights come up
on the black pit town.
Somebody said, "What's a better thing to do?"
Well, it's not just me, and it's not just you,
this is all around the world.

Out in the Indian Ocean, somewhere,
there's a former army post,*
abandoned now, just like the war.
There's no doubt about it,
it was the myth of fingerprints,
that's what that old army post was for.

Well, the sun gets bloody,
and the sun goes down,
ever since the watermelon.
And the lights come up
on the black pit town.
Somebody said, "What's a better thing to do?"
Well, it's not just me, and it's not just you,
this is all around the world.

Over the mountain, down in the valley,
lives the former talk show host,
far and wide his name was known.
He said, "There's no doubt about it,
it was the myth of fingerprints.
That's why we must learn to live alone."

*on Diego Garcia Island

The City of New Orleans

Ridin' on The City of New Orleans,
Eleanor central, Monday morning rail,
fifteen cars and fifteen restless riders,
three conductors, twenty five sacks of mail.
All along the southbound odyssey,
the train pulls out of Kankakee,
and rolls along past houses, farms and fields.
Passing trains that have no name,
and graveyards full of old black men,
and the graveyards of the rusted automobiles.

(chorus)

Good morning, America, how are ya?
Said, don't you know me, I'm your native son?
I'm the train they call The City of New Orleans,
I'll be gone five hundred miles when the day is done.

Dealin' card games with the old man in the club car,
penny a point, ain't no one keepin' score.
Pass the paper bag that holds the bottle,
feel the wheels rumblin' 'neath the floor.
And the sons of Pullman porters,
and the sons of engineers,
ride their fathers' magic carpets made of steel.
Mothers with their babes, asleep,
rockin' to the gentle beat,
and the rhythm of the rails is all they feel.

(chorus)

Night time on The City of New Orleans,
changin' cars in Memphis, Tennessee,
halfway home, we'll be there by mornin',
through the Mississippi darkness,
rollin' down to the sea.
But all the towns and people seem
to fade into a bad dream,
and the steel rail still ain't heard the news.
The conductor sings his songs again:
"The passengers will please refrain."
This train got the disappearin' railroad blues.

Good night, America, how are ya?
Said, don't you know me, I'm your native son?
I'm the train they call The City of New Orleans,
I'll be gone five hundred miles when the day is done.

CHAPTER TWO

Patch Hell a Mile

Ted Torgersen

Patch Hell a Mile

I guess it's time I got around to tellin' this story, so I don't forget, though I ain't the only one heard it, or could do it, or even the only one left that's in it. But I'm tellin' it like I heard it, from the outsider's point of view, don'tcha know.

Anyway, this story took place after the war but before '49, when I was born. I guess you figured out it was an old man tellin' this by now. After the war, like I said, seems like there's always a war goin' on somewhere, or one comin', or they still cleanin' up the mess from the last one, an' it's still like that today, way I see it. Anyway, this war I was talkin' about, I already mentioned that, was the one everybody in them days loved so much, I guess 'cause after it was over people went back to work and there was things for them to do and money to pay them with. It was important then, same as now, since before that money was hard to come by, way I heard it. I guess that's why when I was a boy everybody loved that war so much. Never could see it, myself, but there it is, people went back to work and that's why.

These fellas I'm tellin' you about had a plumbin' outfit in them days, and was on a job that day like everybody else them days, seein' as how there was plenty of work, finally. They was all relatives of mine which is how I know about this, but that's another story. Anyway, part of the job, not all of it, now I never said that, but I was just a boy when I first heard about it, an' that was a long time ago I heard it told the first time. Part of the job, like I said, was a cracked sewer line under the driveway, which meant diggin' it up some to fix the leak. Now, sewer pipe in them days was still cast iron and everybody figured they had enough layin' around the back of the truck to fix it. 'Cept for the blacktop they needed to fix the driveway when they was done, and someone said there might be a few sacks of cold patch back at the shop an' they talked about that. Well, no one liked the idea of usin' cold patch anyways, this bein' a nice neighborhood, and it bein' modern times an' all, hell, after the war, an' cold patch 'ould stand out like sloppy work and no one wanted that. 'Sides they allowed as how they wasn't enough left at the shop and nobody wanted to go back there 'till the job was finished, anyhow.

Now, they had two trucks on the job that day, and since Buzz showed up late, he volunteered to be the one to go for the blacktop, said he heard last night about a pavin' job some fellas was gettin' a day's work outta if he could only remember where, it was a long night. So he took the pickup, an' as he was pullin' away, Walter, his father, yelled "Hey, you forgot the shovel!" but it was too late. I think I already said there was two trucks, the other bein' a panel truck, dark blue, with Chapman Bros. Heating and Cooling on the side, where they kept their tools. Anyway, with Buzz gone without the shovel, that meant there was two t' dig up the driveway and find the leak. Way things went, Ches and Wally started diggin' in opposite directions, with Walter to spell them if need be, Buzz bein' gone with the pickup an' Bud wasn't there, he was still a kid hangin' 'round the firehouse. Was Walter found it right off, I reckon it wasn't his brother he was spellin' that time, and after a short break they got what they needed and fixed the pipe where it was broke in one place and startin' to crack in another. I guess you know everbody's name was there now, 'cept for mine, but like I said, I wasn't born yet, and that's another story.

After they got the trench cleaned out an' the pipe fixed the right way, to last, there was nothin' left to do but wait for the truck to come back an' that's what they did. After a while they started to get the fidgets, an' took turns goin' to the store to get somethin' to help pass the time. Coulda been any one of them went an' got what everyone wanted, but they took turns to pass the time an' in case they seen somethin' extra, seems like everybody had some money in their pocket them times, after the war everybody seemed to love so much, but I already said that.

Anyway, Buzz finally come back about the time the rest of them gave up, but when they seen the way the truck was ridin', said looks like he got enough to patch, hell, a mile. Wonder why he took so long, but he's back now, sure brung enough, too. They was all waitin' for him to back up to the job when they noticed he was asleep at the wheel. You naturally had to expect that, 'cause he had faintin' spells from time to time, though I don't think that's what this was. Now, I remember hearin' them say there was a shovel in the back of the truck that didn't look like one they had seen before, and naturally there was some talk about that. Anyway, it wasn't long before they got the wheelbarrow outta the panel truck and tamped some fresh blacktop in the hole with a pinch bar. When it was full, they drove over it a few times to pack it an' that was that. There was still light in the sky, but not much, when they finished, an' everybody wondered what took Buzz so long, but they was glad the job was finally done and they could go home. They decided right then not to worry about Buzz, he looked so peaceful an' all, 'sides everyone knew he didn't get much sleep, if any, last night, way I heard it. They figured it was a good day 'cause the job was finished and they would get paid, nothin' wrong with that.

Now you dastn't look for too much in this, 'cause I just told it like I heard it, but the talk had it that Buzz made a few stops 'fore he got where he was goin'. I guess a few of them was the same places he was last night but they never said, and there it is. Make a long story short, he found out there was a big pavin' outfit doin' a job nearby and they could use all the help they could get. No one ever said who was runnin' things, I guess everyone knew, or knew better than to ask, way things was in them days. I did hear them say that the boss won't be in, and later people started sayin' he won't be back, go figure. So Buzz went to the job and saw a friend of his, guy who usually built houses outta wood, didn't normally do foundations or paving, just a tradesman pickin' up a day's work where he could. That's the way it generally was back in the days of free enterprise: from each according to his abilities, unto each according to his needs. Some philosopher or other said that. Anyway, his buddy leant him a shovel an' he said he'd bring it back when he was done with it and off he went. The rest you already heard about, mostly from me, 'cept the part where Buzz woke up after dark and everybody was gone. The shovel was still there, 'long with most a the blacktop so he drove to where his friend was workin', but everybody'd left already. There was nothin' for it but to unload the truck an' return the shovel later, which is what he done. Then, he decided to take a few days off. Last I heard it, there was still a shovel in back of the truck and a pile by the side of the road 'cause the pavin' job was done by the time he got back.

Anyway, my time is about done, so I thought I'd write this again, so you wouldn't forget how things was back then, after the war. I hear someone finally came and got the blacktop to build their driveway. I never did hear no more about the shovel, though one day somebody left one in the back of my truck at the fish house, so I guess that turned out alright too. Life is a journey, someone said, an' I'm comin' to the last mile now, myself. What with all the traffic, I hear they's a few rough spots ahead an' I aim to smooth things out a mite 'fore I go. I know they's enough in the back of the truck, an' a shovel, too, to get me where I'm goin'. I guess you could say they left me enough to patch the high road to hell a mile, at least.

———————

Ted Torgersen

Segue

Evil mutants,
with evil minds,
ask me questions
all the time.
I ain't got answers,
I ain't got time.
They won't say
what's really mine.

You, there, lyin'
on the shelf,
go on, say somethin'
about yourself.
Things ain't even,
they're not that way.
Why you ain't got
more to say?

Money's dirty,
so's the game.
Don't ask me nothin',
don't say my name.
How much more
is left to say?
Ask me later,
not today.

You can't tell me
where I been.
I ain't goin'
there again.

More's the pity,
it's just a shame,
far as I know
it's still the same.

Time's right now,
it seems that way.
Don't you believe
I'm here to stay?
What comes after
we start again?
Don't say nothin'
'till the end.

———————————

A' Them Gone

Hear me when I say
there is something here today,
and there can be no peace
'till it's gone,
gone away,
and only we left
here to stay.
Here today,
I gotta say,
there ain't nothin'
in the way.
A' them gone,
yes, they gone,
gone away.

(chorus)

Aaa aa aaa
mm aaa aa aa
A' them gone,
gone away,
yes they gone,
gone to stay.
A' them gone,
yes, they gone,
gone away.
Aaa aa aa aaa
aaa aa aa (etc.)

I may be jumpin' the gun,
as I stand beneath the sun,
but I know there
is no other way.
Why, you want to know,
I been goin'
quite so slow,
as the world seems
to turn another way?
The answer's in your heart,
and it means a brand new start,
the rest of it is still just a lie.
They said it's all in fun,
but now that we've begun,
they gone,
yes, they gone,
they gone away.

(chorus)

I've wondered for too long,
what else can go wrong,
but I have to let the game finish play.
And now here I stand,
knee deep in sand,
as the Arena, it
starts to wash away.
And the blood on the strand
was left there by no man,
so it must have been
some other way.
Are they gone?
Hear me song:
yes, it's true
they have moved on.
Gone away,
yes, they gone,
gone away.

(chorus)

Somewhere near to me
there stands a lemon tree,
and it bears seven leaves
that I can see.
Now they're knocking
on my door,
and they're saying something more,
but I'm tired,
and I just cannot stay.
Older, I get,
but I don't know
nothin' yet.
Just tell me when
they all have gone away.
Gone away, gone away,
they all have gone away.
A' them gone,
yes, they gone,
gone away.

(chorus)

It's something outta reach,
like a carcass on the beach,
but tomorrow
is still another day.
Tell me, so I know,
there's a long way to go,
even if it seems
the other way.
Now I've handed it along,
and you have to sing the song:
gone away,
gone away,
they gone away.

A' them gone,
gone away,
only we are here to stay.
Yes, they gone,
a' them gone,
gone away.

(chorus)

Now, the enemy within
lies just below the skin,
but they left
sometime late yesterday.
Now there's nothin'
left to say,
alla them have gone away.
They gone,
yes, they gone,
gone away.
They must have
heard my song,
war drums beatin'
for so long,
and they still playin' far away.
So they gone,
yes, they gone:
stick and stay,
make it pay.
Yes, they gone,
a' them gone,
they gone away.

(chorus)

———————

Mines and Factories

As I'm thinkin' these thoughts,
I'm takin' my time,
goin' back to the mines,
and factories in my mind.

Yes, goin' back to the mines,
and factories there in my mind.

We gotta get goin'.
It's like wadin' through mud.
Don't like getting' stuck here,
any more than I should.

A weight is upon me,
let's just call it strife.
I can never say nothing,
it's that kind of life.

With each careful step,
you best know the way.
One small mistake and
it's forever you stay.

Now, you heard when I said
that you're wastin' your time,
goin' back to the mines,
and factories of your mind.

The mines and the factories,
that are there all the time.

So I watch where I'm goin',
and lose track of the time,
when I go back to the factories,
and mines in my mind.

Yes, back to the factories,
and mines of my mind.

———————————

Careful Man

I'm a careful man,
with a careful mind,
thinkin' careful thoughts,
most of the time.
All right.
It's a careful song,
it's the song in my heart.
Just think about it,
and we'll each do our part.
All right.
It's the song that we're singin'.
Tonight.

All right.
It's a careful time.
All right.
You gotta know your mind.
All right.
Just you keep on tryin'.
All right.
And we'll figure it out.
Tonight.

Careful, man,
watch where you're goin'.
Careful, man,
it's somethin' worth knowin'.
Keep on the beat,
don't get lost in the heat,
and remember to stay on your feet.
All right.

You don't have to compete
for the kindness you meet,
everything's already complete.
Tonight.

All right.
It's a careful time.
All right.
Know what's in your mind.
All right.
No sense in cryin',
just keep on tryin',
and we'll figure it out
tonight.

I'm a careful man,
and I see what's comin'.
I'm feelin' the beat,
and the drums keep drummin'.
All right.
We're playin' it so careful
tonight.

There's so much to see
in the song of the breeze,
and the light on the evening sea.
All right.
I'm just takin' it easy,
tonight.
Finally, things are alright;
in the breeze from the sea,
it's a reason to be,
and soon comes the morning light.

All right.
Have a careful time.
All right.
Make the most of your mind.
All right.
If you keep on tryin',
all right,
we'll figure it out.
Tonight.

———————

Vision from Outside

I got left so far out there,
I had to reach for my hands.
I heard all the stories, and
they just made me feel bad.
Weren't you careful, like
you meant to be righteous,
and filled up with time;
and while the fire was burning,
you sifted the ashes so fine?
The words that she wrote there
are still etched in my mind,
like a long lazy daydream
that's there all the time:
I remembered that I came
from a world left behind.

The vision from outside,
of what's comin' next,
questions, not answers,
like a right with no left:
my heart's on the inside,
and it's beatin' still,
like a view from no direction,
at the top of the hill.

Better and faster, the way they marched in,
speakin' names and numbers,
and words that never been,
echoin' the thunder that comes by surprise,
remindin' us of the question
she asked with her eyes.
See life from the outside
and remember we tried:
in the simplest things, you see
that the way to be free,
is by keepin' kindness in your mind.

Kindness in your mind…
(repeat).

Breakin' Chain

Ask me somethin',
but not my name,
the rain keeps fallin'
on these dusty claims.
Shackled be me foot, them,
though it seems in vain.
Grace a see me through it,
until they break them chains.

Desire makes a man to be
whatever that he can.
Chain his heart
to keep him hopin',
so he'll make a stand.
Ask me not who cast
them shackles on my soul.
Instead ask yourself, but why,
I must die before I'm old.

Break them chains
with footsteps taken,
forward se'f the day.
Break them chains
with the answers
they dastn't let you say.
More they try to
hold them back,
the more we make them pay.
The seed of truth
frees up the heart,
an' them shackles
fall away.

The roots of greed and ignorance
run long, but never deep.
The sound of chains a breakin'
go make the wicked weep.

The tree of life bears bitter fruit,
make no mistake 'bout that.
'Tis a familiar feelin',
like the rain upon your back.

I hear them chains a breakin'
on the pathway to the sea.
The chains they are a breakin',
so that a' we can be free.
Save the hold of fear and darkness,
them shackles fall away.
They can no longer hide
the truth from the light of day.
Break chain so softly and behold,
them shackles fall away.
Break them chains for all of us,
watch them shackles fall away.

Strange Beans

Stranger than beans, they was,
as they came out of the night.
I couldn't see half a them,
try as I might.
They actin' so careful,
as they took a rest,
tryin' to look normal,
they doin' they best.

Draw up the curtains and
draw down your guns.
We gotta be wary:
you can't know what comes.
Wind at the window and
draught at the door.
I thought I just saw one,
there still could be more.

Orion, the Hunter, with his heavy club,
can't even see them unless they's enough.
I wish that I had it,
it would make things alright.
Maybe then I'd stop hearin' them,
movin' by in the night.

Morning comes soon, but
the shutters are drawn.
Can you still see them
in the early light of dawn?
It would be somethin'
I never seen before,
like when I looked in the oven
and saw apple cores.

Why do I feel that
the world's such a mess?
I fold up my pencils,
and hope for the best.
Life sure is a mystery,
things ain't what they seem,
if they's some reason,
it's stranger than beans.

Outland

I'm not mad, I'm even,
and it's bound to seem odd,
I don't know nothin' about it,
so help me, God.

The cards are playin',
makin' hands by themselves.
A clock on the wall says
a quarter to twelve.

So, how much trouble
you think it's worth?
Now, that was your question,
but I asked you first.

Ain't no worries,
if you take your time,
seein' 'bout yours,
I'm seein' 'bout mine.

Together is a road
that you walk, yourself.
If you ask me about it,
I'll say somethin' else.

Go on, get ready,
It's the start of the show.
I don't know nothin'
that you need to know.

So, don't get mad, be even,
and help level the road.
The fog's on the water
and the nights are cold.

———————————

Ted Torgersen

Lose Them Shoes Blues

My feet are so dusty,
I need some sand in my shoes.
Guess I'll keep walkin',
even though it's no use.
Horizon's in the distance,
nothin' else in my mind,
dirt, must and trouble
followin' closely behind.

The wolf's at my window,
the dog at my door.
I left through the cellar,
couldn't take any more.
Now I'm walkin' these miles,
and nothin' hears my tread,
my feet do the talkin',
nothin' wrong with my head.

I'm rememberin' back when
I was a boy on the beach,
didn't know nothin',
it was all outta reach.
Words are explosive,
like a bomb with a fuse,
blow me clean outta here,
with no more to lose.

So I just keep on walkin',
I'm getting' tired of this;
had enough of the horseshit,
it's so hit or miss.
Man is a dreamer,

just livin' a lie,
can't keep his own custom,
an' don't even know why.

Since I been around here,
there's no shoes on my feet.
They started gettin' heavy
soon as I left the street.
Now my life's on a shoestring,
always comin' untied.
I won't stay in one place,
an' don't even know why.

Though it's hard on my feet,
I gotta keep up the grind.
Ain't noplace I'm goin',
got travelin' on my mind.
And though I keep movin',
I ain't hard to find.
They's no sand in my shoes
since I left them behind.

Life never was easy,
ever since it began.
Try and get over it,
and save what you can.
It has to mean somethin',
though it upsets my mind:
ain't no sand in my shoes
since I left them behind.
True Lies

Truer lies were never spoke:
don't do me no favors,
don't tell me no jokes.
You laugh at my questions

alla the time,
ain't no truth
in your mind.

Over and over,
you sound the same.
All your stories
drive me insane.
Truth is silent,
there you go again,
the lies you tellin'
never end.

What you seen
and where it went,
how much they got,
and what you spent.
I sit and listen
to all these lies,
you hide the truth
behind your eyes.

How many times
I been hearin' this?
You, tellin' me what
I might have missed.
Words and music
playin' in my brain,
lies and truth
keep changin' names.

People starvin' for the truth,
all 'cross the country,
among the youth.
All they hearin'
is your lies.
You just the devil,
in disguise.

It's the foggiest summer
I ever seen,
nobody can tell me
what it means.
Answer's up there
in the sky:
it might not rain
but it's gotta try.

Now we're gettin'
near the end,
summer's gone,
she'll come again.
Evening's spreading
across the land,
the truth is out,
now what's the plan?

Gone A'ready

Gone a'ready,
gone a'ready,
try and understand.
I'm gone a'ready,
gone a'ready,
catch me if you can.

Only once was
something tried for,
something close to me,
the more it comes,
the less is in it,
if only I could see:
it's gone a'ready,
gone a'ready,
like the rest of me.

Time keeps comin',
like it wants to,
wasted, never free.
Love is one thing,
hate another,
both are part of me.
But, I'm gone a'ready,
gone a'ready,
gone a'ready, too.

Another thought
will come tomorrow,
saying nothing true.
But the warning
went for nothing,
it's gone a'ready, too.
Yes, I'm gone,
gone a'ready,
gone a'ready,
gone a'ready, too.

Springtime sends
a savage beauty,
at times it's
nothing new.
Gone a'ready,
gone a'ready,
gone a'ready, too.
Like the sunshine
after moonrise,
it's a world I never knew.
It's gone a'ready,
gone a'ready,
and I'm gone a'ready, too.

Ted Torgersen

Winter comes but
once a lifetime,
and stays forever, too.
'Till it comes,
I dream of summer,
now that's gone
a'ready through.
Nations rise
as shadows fall,
it comes a'ready,
hear the call.
Now they're gone,
there's nothing new.
Gone a'ready,
gone a'ready,
yes, they gone
from me and you.

But I'm gone a'ready,
gone a'ready,
gone a'ready, too.
So don't wait no longer,
it just gets stronger,
and weakens what I do.
'Till I'm gone a'ready,
gone a'ready,
gone a'ready, too.
Yes, I'm gone,
it's comin' true.
Gone a'ready,
gone a'ready,
gone a'ready through.

Make me stay here
for a long time,
remember what I do.
Waiting longer,
but no stronger,
I'm gone a'ready too.
Yes, I'm gone without it,
never doubt it,
gone a'ready,
gone a'ready,
gone a'ready too.

Mind revealing,
not self serving,
we're only just a few.
Why, there's nothing,
for no reason,
'cept what
I couldn't do.
But I don't remember
how I came here,
it's gone a'ready, too.
Yes, I'm gone a'ready,
gone a'ready,
gone a'ready, too.

Gone a'ready,
gone a'ready,
try and understand.
That I'm gone a'ready,
gone a'ready,
catch me if you can.

Rain Time

My epitaph's on my tombstone,
an' I think it's gonna rain,
the words there are half written,
an' I think it's gonna rain.
The things that you said to me
are still drivin' me insane:
that I'm goin' to another place
where no one knows my name.
Yes, I believe it's comin' on to rain.

I think that I'm in trouble,
I think that's what you said,
they ain't gonna find my words,
'cause I wrote these instead.
My time ain't good for nothin',
it's as empty as my head,
I got a real, real problem
'cause my tombstone says I'm dead.
I know it's gonna cost me somethin',
that I ain't paid for yet.

Yes, I believe, I believe it's gonna rain.
Wishin' ain't gonna stop it,
the sky is lookin' strange:
yes, I see that it's comin' on to rain.
Yes, I believe it's comin' on to rain.

I was sleepin' in the parlor,
dreamin' 'bout a train,
someone was leanin' on the whistle,
like they was tryin' to stop the pain.
Yes, I believe it's comin' on to rain.
Foxfire 'cross the swampland,
clouds that hide the moon,
all the signs that I'm seein'
say the rain is comin' soon.
Yes, I believe it's comin' on to rain.

A miracle takes some doin',
there's an idea in my brain,
somethin' that keeps on goin',
like the water down the drain.
Yes, I believe it's comin' on to rain.
I see that it's makin' up to rain.

The storm I seen a comin',
no one ever seen the like.
The pressure keeps on fallin',
and there's nothin' here to like.
The rain won't stop a comin'
'till the world is wringin' wet.
I guarantee, from what I see,
there ain't been nothin' like this yet.
Yes, I believe it's gonna rain.
Yes, I believe it's comin' on to rain.

More and more it's comin',
it's floodin' 'cross the plain.
People ain't goin' nowhere,
an' I believe it's gonna rain.
Yes, I believe, I believe it's gonna rain.

Hear me good and listen,
the rain is comin' soon.
I guess I heard about it
in the darkness of the moon.
Yes, I believe it's comin' on to rain.
The voices are all quiet,
the words are in my head.
If it amounts to something,
I ain't thought about it yet.
An' I believe it's comin' on to rain.
Yes, I believe it's comin' on to rain.

The Unknowable

Back at the time things started,
everything was already there.
But you could only see a part of it,
or was it that you just didn't care?
Outside of what you're a part of,
and what you think you can learn,
something's out there still waiting,
like a fire waiting to burn.

I listened one time to a preacher,
who talked about Heaven and Hell.
I found I couldn't quite understand him,
and whatever he was trying to sell.
In a hole a man stands, shovel in hand,
does that mean he's digging a well?
What if he got it all backwards,
and Hell is where heroes must go?
And Heaven don't care, 'cause you're already there:
it's something you never could know.

Could you somehow find out what's coming,
by thinking outside where you're at?
Trouble and woe you already know,
must it be something like that?
Or could it be that the sky wasn't cloudy,
and now it's raining and you don't have a hat.
You wear yourself out, looking about,
when there never was anything to doubt.

———————————

Land Shark

Weevils are in the flour
and the ants are everywhere;
I got no money in my pocket,
and I'm about to lose my hair.
Land shark.
Keeps doin' this to me,
land shark,
tearin' this world apart,
land shark,
and causin' so much misery;
land shark,
just won't let things be
the way they were meant to be.

Every time I look around
there's something new to see,
peace of mind, it's out of time,
he's on a shopping spree.
It's plain to see, for you and me,
all the sharks ain't in the sea.
Land shark.

He's buyin' up spare parts,
        land shark,
and he's sellin' every hope.
    Land shark:
he's buyin' picture postcards,
an' he's peddlin' enough rope,
        land shark.

    Keeps doin' this to me,
        land shark,
tearin' this world apart,
        land shark,
and causin' so much misery;
        land shark,
    just won't let things be
the way they were meant to be.

    My oh my, I wonder why
    he's eatin' up the land.
I wonder how it's gonna be
with everything in his hands.
    Land shark.
He can see you in the dark,
        land shark,
he's got no reason to be fair,
        land shark,
'bout the seasons and the air.
    He's a land shark,
    eatin' up the place,
        land shark,
stealin' away your face,
        land shark.

I went to lay my cards down,
now that they're all in one place;
I looked up to find out
that he'd eaten every ace.
Land shark.
Don't you hear what I am sayin',
land shark?
Don't ya know,
they're the cards we been a playin',
land shark?
It's the world we livin' in,
land shark,
back to the beginnin',
land shark.
I got me a notion,
land shark,
to heave you in the ocean,
land shark,
and let you eat for free.
I saw an early moonrise,
all the rain had blown away.
Tonight, the stars are shinin' bright,
and tomorrow's a brand new day.
Land shark.
He's gaspin' out his last.
Land shark:
right now he's sinkin' fast,
land shark.
From these windows by the sea,
it's finally clear to me,
that he was never meant to be:
land shark.

———

Tent Rentals

I went down to the campground,
and tried to rent a tent.
The place by the sea, where
all those times had been spent.

They mustered after me and they sent
out all they got. Instead, I asked them,
say, what have you that is not?
A place where I might go and rent a tent.

A tent, they said, a tent.
Go rent yourself a tent.
A place to stay and a place to keep,
I guess that's all they meant,
but I took it somewhat differently
when they said "go rent a tent."

Have you any soldiers,
to go marching off to war?
They've taken most of what you've got,
can you spare them any more?
A foul river runs this way,
bending round about.
Think it knows, the way it goes,
it's rotten to the core?

All I did was come here,
and look to rent a tent.
The good times and the bad times
had already been spent.
But my intent was never bent,
I guess that's what it meant.
I tented, I rented, I rented a tent.
A tent, a tent, a tent.
I came and rented a tent, a tent.
Rented a, rented a tent.

On the ragged edge of nowhere,
pitched for miles in endless rows,
they dwell in utter mindlessness,
and around them nothing grows.
Long lasts eternity, the downtime of the stars:
I think I'll spend the rest of mine
on the iron plains of Mars.

———————

Men in Grey Suits

Look where you goin',
before you go out.
They must be there somewhere,
no'n' but teet' in they mout'.

Step into the Arena,
where everything counts,
where it's decided
what's up and who's out.

Now the sky's getting'
as dark as the sea.
Was he lookin' at you?
Is he still after me?

Fins cuttin' the water,
as they circle about,
don't look behind you,
there's never a doubt.

Swim to the shallows
and stand on the shore.
Be glad that you got here,
they can't get you no more.

Lunchtime's for losers,
they servin' just now.
Try it in roti,
it's better, some how.

Think while you eatin',
what this is about.
Reckon they ain't nothin'
but teet' in they mout'.

———————————

Ted Torgersen

Turtle and Shark

Look there, on the water,
they no longer apart.
They swim together,
turtle and shark.

Brothers then fought here,
diff'rent sides make you say:
take what they teach you,
learn it some way.

They always together,
it ain't a sky lark.
They swim forever,
turtle and shark.

A' we sail the deep,
wit' we brethren on the ark.
They came here before we,
did turtle and shark.

Mankind's just tearin'
this old world apart.
It's not even a memory,
to turtle and shark.

There's no tomorrow,
'cept through the heart:
they swim together,
turtle and shark.

Now that it's over,
an' it's just getting' dark,
we ain't goin' nowhere,
'cept wit' turtle and shark.

After We Are Weevils

Make you say something,
you know, don't forget.
Say why you came here,
it's a' you might get.

Green gettin' long time,
there's dry times ahead.
Why is it like this?
Is it somethin' I said?

Dry time's a comin',
I think, say, I said.
Why don't you get it?
What's wrong with your head?

These are the dry times,
the rain comes at noon.
Cry tears and laughter,
just hope it comes soon.

After we are weevils,
they baked in we bread.
Ask me 'bout it sometime,
and remember we dread.

Crapaud Smoke He Pipe

A' you come to see the circus,
and now it's nearly night.
The elephant a'ready here,
crapaud smoke he pipe.

All a gone get ready,
they hold, se'f, no more show.
The air is really heavy,
I thought you'd like to know.

That's what they complain about,
I guess it's just they gripe.
Elephant was made like that,
crapaud smoke he pipe.

There's nothing left to stop we now,
t'ings been set a'right.
What them do no bother,
crapaud smoke he pipe.

Them try for take 'way everything,
I guess you know the type.
Elephant ain't light enough,
crapaud smoke he pipe.

Glass Snapper

Hear, a' you boatmen,
when you go to sea,
if you hold glass snapper,
no bring 'e to me.

Me no want glass snapper,
'e bright in he eye.
Pitch a to the cobbler
up there in the sky.

Now they pullin' glass snapper,
twenty head to the string.
I just come here lately,
never seen such a thing.

Cook when you come shore,
make you try it out.
No mind how you fix it,
it taste bad in your mout'.

Loose a' the rope from
co'nut tree where he stay;
pole a meet sand,
kingfish comin' today.

Now bring me glass snapper,
he eye turnin' black.
Don't you dast keep a,
just t'row 'e back.

The End of the Road

Most promises are empty,
like the space between the stars.
Who am I, that comes this way,
to tell you where you are?

Mankind knows but troubles,
empty times fill your life;
you kill yourselves and others
with all this hopeless strife.

The answer stands before you all.
Your voice says "but a child?"
Loose the times and never mind,
the wolf is running wild.

Is there any recompense
for all that's gone before?
The more, you think, you smell the stink
that's come to your front door.

Deny it entry, ignore its call,
nothing of it can save you all
from half the misery in sight.
It walks in the absence of light.

Fog crawls through the walls,
clouds just hide the sun;
the smoke of forests burning
say: you'll never see it done.

Then, meanwhile, in the corridors,
the endless place that knows no time,
your brains, themselves, run down the drain.
Was there something on your mind?

Mist is hiding heavy costs,
in a world already lost.
Payback is only bought,
for a penny, in your thoughts.

Nobody sees the future, it comes like it must.
On wings of storm it flattens your corn,
and lays waste to all the rest.
Time for planting's over,
the storm made such a mess.
Reaping's done, clouds cover the sun,
and the world is buried in dust.

Ashes from the fire, grey,
like the image in your mind;
mankind didn't last that long,
and mostly just wasted time

———————

The Keeping of the Cat

Why you t'ink you mind him?
It never was like that.
The land is just a mystery,
i' the keeping of the cat.

He knows the way to walk there,
he knows just when to pounce.
It's given him to keep it,
why t'ink say name him ounce?
The way was ever caution,
but, say you, what of that?
The world he knew was ever mine,
i' the keeping of the cat.

Why, se'f, you no see him,
is he still as big as that?
Life is but a debt I pay
i' the keeping of the cat.

Say he has a short tail,
proverbs in your mout'.
Make you don't see nothin'
that this is all about?

Snow lies on the river,
ice beneath your hat.
Water's just a state of mind,
i' the keeping of the cat.

Dragon breathes but fire,
the land, it is what stays.
'Fore day mornin', as it was,
ancient, like our days.

What of this new morning?
You heard about a' that.
It's just another day,
i' the keeping of the cat.

All a you must hear the call,
an' see about a' that.
The world is as it ever was,
i' the keeping of the cat.

———————

Water Waits

I only drink the water,
I guess it's about time.
Let it out, spare the doubt,
don't leave yourself behind.

Time thinks it's makin' money,
for others of it's kind.
Water waits, don't be late,
or you'll muck it up this time.

My glass, it's half empty.
See if you can make it spin.
Pour something in, it tastes like gin,
it's poison to your mind.

Water waits beneath your feet,
where brave men fear to tread.
Take a drink of water, and
make you keep your dread.

Thirsty, they search for water,
sometimes it's hard to find.
The wind from the land wrinkled the sand,
was that why they crossed the line?

Water waits for all of us,
deep or shoal, make up your mind.
What you need is on the reef,
it's out of reach this time.

Water waits for nothing,
the mill it grinds real fine.
They already drank all theirs up,
and now they want most of mine.

Water waits, behind locks and gates,
to wash away the grime.
Turn it loose, it's just no use,
in a world of ooze and slime.

———————————

Aerie

Word from the nest
flies quick as a thought:
man looks for something,
it cannot be bought.
And if it's somewhere,
in a sky so free,
then when he finds it,
what happens to me?
Fly's safe in the web,
but he ain't stayin' long.
Time Anansi gets back,
I will be gone.

You all know the answer,
but it might make you cry.
Everyone knows that
eagles can't fly.
It means more to me now,
but I won't tell you why.
It starts with the beginning,
it may never end,
break as often as you have to,
but don't you dast bend.

Now you know the story,
you have heard it all;
crapaud ain't lookin'
at the fly on the wall.
Spider is sleepin',
bird's in the sky.
Learn to laugh
at yourself,
and I'll
teach you to fly.

Duty Calls

As the good horse starts
at the shadow of the lash,
so the good ox pulls the plow
by day, 'till he's heart burst,
and without breaking stride,
continues to plow jumbe furrows
in the wan moonlight.

Time and tides, cycles that never cease,
bring back the beginning of things
from the ashes on the heap.
The herd gathers, as willows
bend in the sere breeze,
scenting water in a dry land,
their blood's moisture,
like nature's imperative,
calling up a thirst
that cannot be slaked.
They follow the monkey light,
seeking the source,
it's promise luring them
into the mire,
like cones that lie where
they drop and await the fire.
More fools we who wait
for a sweet smell:
the fresh breeze
that enters Hell's gate.

A Mild Comparison

I keep on swearin' these petty venganzas,
for them whose time was before mine,
for those simple, small things buried,
that they dance upon at the end of time.

Were the course of humanity righteous,
and at last somehow answered the call,
in time to make some sense of this,
the emptiness that waits for you all.
Can't it ever be seen, even in your dreams,
that mankind must first learn to crawl?

You who are high and mighty,
big people and all them,
have made what means about nothing,
like the branches on the stem.
Attack the roots of ignorance,
and everything falls away;
see that ants and cockroaches
have carried evolution's day.

We who stand firm
'gainst the conqueror worm,
see them crawl through
along the way.
And in every day, in every way,
it's getting better and better.

Bottom Feeding Suction Eels

A spate of madness follows
rational thought, a long time thinking,
each moment, bought with a penance
for your thoughts in these here easy times:
make up your mind. Notion or motion,
they scramble through a nation of masonry,
bricks and sticks, sold like
the trees, overseas, shattered like dreams,
without even a by your leave.

How have I told you, let me
count the ways. They get the wind up,
we're left with the count down.
Battles offered me, bottles in front
of me, better than a frontal lobotomy.
I gone to the village for a bottle
of tequila, got to get the rum
out of me system. Perhaps that
and a jar of tamarind pickles.

Fickle hates finger their plan,
as they hide themselves in the ooze,
every one a them in the shape of a man.
They know they can't lose,
'cause nothing of theirs is at stake,
forever dodgin' the rake,
tines in your mind, if only
you could leave them all behind.

Weakness is protection for the strong,
who can still tell right from wrong,
even though they know they stuck with both.
The botheration of blame follows their pain,
like the arrow from the bow, so they
feel that they know where to go.
Don't be fooled, the writers of rules
don't dast answer the questions you ask.
On harmony's stage, their plans are laid,
to trick those who're made in the shadows.
If you face the light, step into their sight,
watch the dust bite back out of fright,
you might see the pain in their empty souls.
How many have died, or lived wasted, useless lives
because they listened to lies, regardless
of size, no hope in their minds or their eyes?

Whispers, you hear, words in your ear, that prey
on your brain, 'till it's gone down the drain,
insane, like memories of early life.
Yet, as you live, you have one thing to give:
your refusal is the something they must take,
though it leaves them naked with their mistakes.
Time to turn the page, at this forsaken stage,
clear minds see us through this benighted age.

Leave the benthic worms and vermin
to their several devices, and in time
they will consume each other. Ha,
so they fool us all the time. Stomp
the shit out of them, don't deal with they folly.
Mankind's round the bend and down the alley,
and to survive, must shed them completely,
free from regret, or awe of their control of history.

Termites

I guess there really was a guy,
    once upon a time.
They called him Tommy Termite,
    I hope he didn't mind.

Carpenters, they built that house,
    I lived there for quite a time;
along came Tommy Termite:
    the world just isn't kind.

They built a lot of houses
    along the high road to Hell.
More than one of them fell down,
'cause of what Tommy came to sell.

Hear the gnawing in the walls,
    as your world yaws to and fro.
Like the others, heed the call:
    take what you can and go.

They called him Tommy Termite,
    he ate just like a mouse.
He always tried to scam the world,
    but he was just a louse.

———————————

Man With No Face

No mind how you wash this,
the words can't come clean.
The road is long and dusty,
scrub it in your dreams.
It weighs more when you toss it,
than it was supposed to mean;
'cause it don't count for nothing,
like the grief in between.

The rulers built this road,
and paved it with our bones.
I walked here just lately,
and it ain't the way home.
You can't, se'f, blame them
for what them a do,
until you done feelin'
the lash through and through.

Massa day done here,
under the sun.
Them that don't know it,
been havin' they fun.
A' we se'f know that
the world's in a state.
All that's behind them now,
save we at the gate.

Plans Are Made

You better have an evil plan,
'cause you know that they have one;
you have to get what belongs to you,
before the getting's done.

They'll hear about the times we lived
in an age so far away;
it don't help us to realize
what we have to do today.

Matter's what ever matters,
I think someone said that twice.
The world's half done,
before we've begun,
between the fire and the ice.

Majesty once spoke to me,
and I heard but the fanfare,
and like a fire in the sun,
the world don't even care.

Our days are numbered, yours and mine:
take the time to travel, no mind what's behind.
Don't stand there in the shadows,
tryin' to guess what price
it's gonna cost us all,
to make things alright twice.

Back Off

I tell them all to back off.
Believe me, I have not
said it once, or in error, but
many are the times
they have come for me.
It will ring unto infinity, what I say,
when I tell them to back off.

Most, if not all, is lost. You know it.
Your spirit screams it.
Those who have gone before you
and died in vain know it well.
But I am not as well.

As long as I cast a shadow,
I am not part of it.
The shadow knows but
of the evil in the hearts of men.
Are you who live not over it?

I am not. I will live until I die,
and never know what lurks there:
in the darkness, the empty place
between the stars, where I go,
where my spirit dwells forever,
until you tell them to back off.

———————————

The Boy

Puer, attend to this,
as you spend your days in strife.
Puer, explain all this,
as you walk the edge of the knife.
As a boy you heard men talk,
and you knew what you knew then.
Speak about it now, and you
know that it's the end.

They tested you most mercilessly,
and the days came and went.
According to the words they mouthed,
all your times have been spent.

You attended the funeral,
the first of several.
The horns on the goat of time
made you the caporal.
Why you, self, saw nothing,
to see you through the night,
bears the mark of betrayal,
that hides behind the light.

At last, time remembers you,
and reveals it's mercurial face.
Now, the words you spoke so long ago
seem to have no place.

———————————

Remember

In the unfortunate cause,
I once sought strength,
but none came.
When everything was given,
I lost myself,
in order to find
the beginning of time
in the simplest of things.
Now, in the face of everything,
I count as nothing.
Gone away,
like the place where she stayed.

Ghost science calls out an answer
on wings of storm.
Begging the question,
it preserves us from harm.
Death precludes harmony,
but life lives itself:
why is it so hard,
your reason asks,
to see, that when
the shadow fell,
it fell on me?

Sons of thunder,
fly your flag.
Life alone, not
the cause, is lost.
Time is out.
In the place
after time, remember:
by the hand
that delivers me,
so shall
I be delivered.

———————————

Jelly Bags

I was cleanin' out my closet,
now there's somethin' in my hand.
It's quite underrated,
you need to understand.

Make a note,
for all these folks,
so they can
take a chance.

Look at what we got here,
it's somethin' from the past.
Ain't no tellin' what it was,
it's surely made to last.

I saw it here this mornin',
it's part of everyone's plan.
No way to do without it,
it's from the industry of man.

There's somethin' here,
that don't appear,
though it's done for everyone.
At your door,
hear the wildness roar,
shut it and still it comes.

Has it any magic,
the way miracles seldom come?
It's here now,
you can't stir it down,
I think it's almost done.

The climate's getting' temperate,
it ain't hard to adjust.
Just think what you want to think,
and do but what you must.

How can I list
what was missed,
from ancient to
modern times?
It's all uphill,
like a worldly thrill,
that's climbin'
through our lives.

Here comes bumpy water,
here come turbulent times:
try to thrive, not just survive,
and open up your mind.

It's all about the way
things were done in olden times:
just do what you gotta do,
and take up what you find.

Monkey on a String

Danger doesn't wait for me,
clap hands, it looks like fun;
I can't even try to get away:
I am the captive one.

Now I hear the music,
and dance until it's done.
All the time I'm thinkin' 'bout
which way I want to run.

Birds have the sky
in which to try,
and escape into the sun.
But I'm just a monkey on a string,
I could be anyone.

No matter who turns the crank,
the music sounds the same.
The cup is full of pennies,
but the monkey has no name.

The evil grinders of my life
always seem to act the same.
They take whatever comes their way,
and leave me here in shame.

Today the rain is fallin',
and I don't pay it any mind.
I seem to dream freedom's dream,
where glory's left behind.

I monkeyin' with madness,
and coverin' up with grime.
Tryin' to escape, myself,
and somehow stop the times.

I drank the cup of knowledge,
and now I know just what it means:
I never had what it takes
for freedom in the trees.

———————————

One Morning

On the morning of this day,
I man slowly walk away,
no more to show you my face.

I now sadly walk away,
you never asked me to stay,
and now I gone from
all the shame and disgrace.

In the ending of our days
things are wrong, like always;
and now at last you send me away.

So I'm gone, gone away,
like the wind from yesterday,
nor will you ever hear
what I did say.

Time has come and gone,
and at last I'm feelin' strong,
no more to listen to your lies.

The truth behind your eyes
is buried, like lost tides,
and the reef is rotting on the sand.

Love has gone away,
and now these songs will play,
for all of those legends and their day.

Like your heart,
your words are cold,
as the lifetime that you sold,
double banded, like the rainbow
of your disguise.

Hide yourself within,
like you did way back then.
Never, again, will you see the day
that you could cloud my mind,
like an afterthought, left behind;
in the morning of your designs
I walk away.

This day brings me grace,
and I'll slowly walk away;
even the dust is dust
where you stay.
Love came here to die,
and leave me behind,
to speak whatever's
left in my mind.

The luck was always bad,
that's what's makin' me so sad.
Better to remember better days.
And everything you said
is still there, in my head,
as I man slowly walk away.

Once more to slide out through the cracks,
this time with nothing at my back,
as ever, I gladly slip away.

———————————

Day of the Beast

It's the day of the Beast,
don't look to the East,
'cause the sun ain't a goin' that way.
I think it's still best
that it goes to the West,
like the songs that we know always say.

It's the day of the Beast,
it just gives me the creeps,
the times, they won't let you be.
So, far into the night,
consider everything twice,
and wonder if it's really alright.

It's the day of the Beast,
it's the day we like least,
better not try to understand.
Everything after seems better and faster,
than things were before it all came.
We waited so long, but now that it's gone,
it won't ever be back here again.
It's the day of the Beast,
and the sellout's complete,
just march to your fate, never mind.
They like things this way,
and no matter what they say,
planned it like this all the time.

It's the day of the Beast,
and whoever you meet,
has already decided your fate.
Though their words sound so strong,
things still come out wrong,
and the date says it's already too late.

So we pull the blue string,
'cause there's still songs to sing,
they couldn't quite stop us this time.
Tell them there's no peace,
it's the day of the Beast,
and we gonna keep speakin' our minds.

Long Eared Devil

The night wind's a blowin', steady and cold,
that long eared devil's got a lien on my soul.
Down in the river bottom, he's startin' his run.
Messin' with my life, yeah, he does it for fun.

Well, I climbed behind the wheel of my Chevy sedan,
I could see him clearly, he was hatchin' a plan,
so I lit outta Dodge, goin' fast as I can.
My foot was getting' tired, I was runnin' outta luck,
when he came up behind me in a hot rod pickup truck.
Flames started shootin' out of the pickup's grill,
but the Deuce, he couldn't catch me,
at the top of the hill.

Now I'm really tired, I been drivin' all night,
keep on lookin' behind me, hopin' it's alright.
My headlights are shinin', lightin' up the ditch,
I see that long eared devil, he's standin' on the bridge.
A steamboat is passin', and he begins to dance,
drawbridge is raisin', there's no way to advance.

I threw that old Chevy right into a skid,
reversed back the way I came, right back up the hill.
I know I'll feel better if I get me some sleep,
forget about this whole long night, my soul to keep.
Next time that devil tries to run me to ground,
I'm gonna pick a place to hide where I can't be found.

That long eared devil seems to know just what I do,
but with the cards that I'm holdin', he's in trouble too.
If I could see things clearly, in the light of day,
I could leave him miles behind me,
no matter what they say.
This time I'm ready for him, I'm easy on my feet,
tonight the cards are on my side, and I got deuces beat.
Outside, the moon is rising, and help is on it's way,
you long eared devil: this time it's Hell you pay.
Now the morning sun is risin',
and nothin' looks the same,
I paid my life's ransom,
and it closed down their game.
Though they keep tryin' to catch me,
keep on baitin' their hooks,
this one time, damn their eyes,
they need to take another look.

———————————

Siwash

You know, I think you're ugly,
I know I'm ugly too.
Grown men run at the sight of me,
and I ain't as ugly as you.

You're ugly as a durn Siwash,
the facts are as plain as that.
The devil, himself, has a much nicer pelt,
and wouldn't wear yours for a hat.

When we were rowin' across Lake Eerie,
you turned all scringey and pale.
This much I know: if the wind started to blow,
I'd hang you, ass up, for a sail.

Note: this poem comes with a Free Money Back Guarantee: you
don't get it free, and you don't get your money back, either, after you
decide you don't like it.

It's Been Long Seen

'Tis with a heart, so dismally,
I walk between your steps;
and remember the time
you showed me,
something never to forget.

Is it to be, for always, like it is?
You on your path, me on mine,
never to feel or regret?

You once showed me the back of you,
but I took it not at all.
Can the wordless things we spoke
ever be answered, or call?

Am I still worth a moment,
stolen from your life?
Or must I just ever crawl,
back over the things
we laughed and talked about,
to stay where I am now?

Remember what I said then,
think of when and how:
remember the horse I said I'd have,
already harnessed to the plow.

Random

Random thoughts on a random page,
random records of a random age,
random diggin's in random mines,
like random portions of random finds;
life seems so random, most of the time,
like random faces, and random crimes,
random stars on random nights,
or random fighters in random fights.
Random devils and their games,
random objects, with random names;
a random shellfish, with a random claw,
random cards in a random draw,
random pains in random teeth,
keep me walkin' on random feet.
Random coffins in random graves,
are like places I visit on random days.
Random targets, random hits,
random feelings, and random fits,
make random rhythms that never quit.
Random truths and random lies
look the same through random eyes.
The random meanings of random lines
tell the same old story, every time.

Caution, to the Winds, No Less

A rhyme needs no reason, not a bit nor a whit;
like freedom's arrow from the bow unstrung,
there's no way to loosen it.
Try as I may to capture the day,
I'm sorry to say, there just isn't a way.
I guess it's time to quit.
Mercy, it needs no fiction
to justify the things that went so wrong.
Come, walk alone, this lonesome road,
the day is nearly done.

You must do something,
say something,
'cause life is not no dream;
it's a one way street,
and every rocket pass,
so, do your last thing fast.

Devil Child

On the eve of all ills,
we took to the hills,
with no light to shine for a guide.
To see us over and on,
and everywhere beyond,
we had the smile
of a Devil Child.

So, make up your mind,
or leave it behind,
steer straight
the course of mankind.
With nowhere behind you
and nothing to guide you
'cept the smile
of a Devil Child.

Through the eyes in our heads,
we're so easily led,
by the smile
of a Devil Child.

See where you've been,
when the music begins,
in the smile
of a Devil Child.

———————

Mr. Fixit Ticket Beats the Devil to Road Town

(chorus)

Drivin' like the devil,
yes, he drivin' like the devil,
drivin' to beat the devil
through the night.

You hear that tap-tap tappin'?
But, ain't nothin' gonna happen,
it's just he fender flappin', it's alright.
He's drivin' to beat the devil,
everywhere the road is level,
he drivin' like the devil in the night.

(chorus)

Goin' past the churchyard,
he drivin' with all he might;
rollin' past the gaol house
in the quiet time of night.
Dayclean, he reach the courthouse steps
in time to stop the fight.
'Fore they tell the magistrate,
he man outta sight.

(chorus)

He drivin' in the daytime,
the way he drove all night.
It's not like he so reckless,
he just want to set t'ing right.

(chorus)

Murder Night

Like a trace of something, almost gone,
shooting across your sight,
without a word to sound its way,
across the long night it goes,
to remind us of the day.
Like a tumbler full of stars,
shaken, not stirred,
poured 'cross the firmament,
not left merely to ferment,
lest we ever forget
the random feelings we still get,
from light on a background of dark.

See the stars, feel the night,
so when morning begins,
you be not blinded
by your inner sight,
and recall that something
was not offered,
so you would embrace the emptiness
that was supposed to be alright.

Traces leave meaning behind,
like a shooting star;
no matter where you started out,
it only matters where you are.
Can we see what cast no shade
upon our troubled lives?
The woe that we will ever know
eclipses us all the time.
Can you count them, no, more,
the spaces between them,
as they spill across your sight?
Though countless be those points of light,
the darkness is where they are.

No mind that refuge, wherever you seek it,
comes without a reason, and,
should you but choose to speak it,
reminds you, even at the last,
that the night is almost past,
and came but to teach us,
that always we must,
for all the days to come,
suffer the light.

Reflection

That's what's interesting about this life, no one ever really trusts anyone, no matter what they say. Think of it, they only trust those they must, and even then, only just the ones that they know they have power over, to make them feel bad, or whatever, anyhow, if they don't get what they want. It surely is a caution, and caution is what makes the world go 'round, as the saying goes.

> Now duck is what I did,
> it was bound to keep me hid,
> I knew I couldn't hide all the waste.
> So I put it in one place,
> and today's a brand new day:
> they'll have to cook my goose another way. Hey!?

Fire seems friendly at times, according to conditions, nights are cold and bones get old. Light one and see, but it's burn yourself burns an you touch it. Light lures the mindless moth, crispy critters that do not flee the truth. Murder the turtles, it might make the mud feel better; otherwise, why do it? It's not what it means to me, it's what I mean to it. Like being caught in a rhyme that won't quit.

> Don't mouse around like this,
> because it's hit or miss,
> in it's nearness.
> (There'll be a short quiz on this later.)

In some cases, much later. Although it seems presumptuous of me so to state: I think so. Remember what you can and forget everything else: a formula for the intellectual progress of our times. So, you see, it is easy after all. Writing is legal as long as you don't get caught, just like the song says.

CHAPTER THREE

Chenrezig

Devil Duck

I once cooked the devil,
in the form of a duck.
Don't matter why I did it,
it brought me good luck.

Now, people tell me
to repent of my crime,
but I don't see the reason,
at least it was mine.

Heave away,
heave away,
do like you're told:
you won't sit by the fire,
'cause you'll never grow old.

Haul away,
haul away,
the ashes are cold,
don't bother to stoke them,
the place has been sold.

Sail away,
sail away,
like you've never been born.
Don't think about it,
you've already been warned.

(Reprise)

I'm the devil,
in the deep blue sea.
I'm the devil,
won't you listen to me.

I'm the devil,
in the bright blue skies.
I'm the devil,
hope you see through my disguise.

Heave away,
heave away,
the sail, it is slack.
Heave away, me brethren,
make you haul it back.

Haul away,
haul away,
light's still left in the sky.
Tomorrow will come,
and you'll be alive.

Sail away,
sail away,
we run 'fore the wind.
Make you empty the bilges
before you turn in.

———————

Mirror

Sing the song named Watergate,
and let the spirit weil;
hear the song of ages play,
feel the scabs
that do not heal.

Rightly, wrongly, so duly, do,
and make but matters worse:
do the thing you feel, at last,
let the world now feel the hurt.

It looks like where we started out,
but it's still a mile behind;
ahead of all the crying, so,
don't pay it any mind.

A golden web of light
shields the maker force
from our sight.
Eyes feed first upon water,
then on air as we breathe.

A tree bends,
rustling to the sun,
saying: leave us,
old winter, leave us.

A man cries first for air.
Then the cruel eyes come,
and he is open.
Finally, Death comes in
with a basket of rainbows.

Ted Torgersen

The House of Trains

He sat there as if he were busy,
and he sat for a long time.
He heard the words
that were spoken all about him,
but he never heard the truth.

There is a time for stillness,
and there is a time to move.
How did he know them, then,
by the days that were gone before?
Or was it something in him,
that drove him to it?

Instead of lamenting
the waning of culture,
he tried his hand at
waxing the moon.

When that didn't work,
he was back at the station,
and he wondered if getting on
was worth it, this time.

———————

The Path of Error

When all the
pretty little horses
are lying, dead,
on a field of dreams,
why are there still some
who take joy
in beating them?

If wishes were horses,
then beggars would ride,
but the seeker
of knowledge
sits quietly,
by the road side.

The seed it is sown.
the curse, it is cast.
For those who
come to eat it,
it's a likely repast.

But the seed of truth,
like the karela,
bears bitter fruit,
at last.

Know Peace

Peace by peace,
a man knows peace,
pieces of himself,
and the puzzle
that is life.

Piece by piece,
he finds himself,
puzzled by
the daughters of memory,
like the peace
that stands by itself.

Life is more than
a series of pieces of meat,
one to be,
and some to eat.
That, alone,
is a piece of peace.

Then, there is war,
and all forms of strife,
with stress as the magnet
that calls you to life.
How, then, can you
know peace?

———————

Desperadoes Make Good Neighbors

Four men, they stood
on the hilltop,
outlined against the sun;
you could know them by
the robes they wore,
desperadoes every one.

The fading light shone,
as if from afar,
as it lit up that foreign shore.
A place for them
to work and live,
a refuge,
yet something more.

If they were many,
and spent their lives
on the run,
would their journey
be over faster?
Come what may,
the truth, it stays,
both then and ever after.

Losar the Canadian

Losar, the Canadian,
came down from the temperate zone,
to arrange a cease fire
between the British or the Americans
and the birds they were shooting
off the telephone wires.
And he walked through
the frozen landscape alone.

"Peace needs War,"
said the horse,
"to keep it by force.
Without war,
there would be
no such thing as peace."

So, if peace needs
war to keep and enforce it,
why all the shouting?
Who is really singing, tonight?

If we can stop them
from shooting
the birds on the wire,
before they fly higher,
and bullets can't reach them,
then they'll have to shoot
themselves or each other
until there are no more of them.
Will that bring peace?

Or was Losar trying to tell us something,
about living in a neutral country,
that we all needed to hear,
but couldn't remember or pronounce?
Constant bombardment
has deafened our ears
to the fact that war can't defend us,
and if we could just start over,
it would be, truly, a New Year.

———————————————

CHAPTER FOUR:

Mongoose Dentist

Mongoose Dentist

I Mongoose Dentist,
rat better watch out.
Make you no show me
the teet' in you mout'.

Even, se'f, you smilin',
an' I take it that way,
hand me them pliers:
today is the day.

Control a' you diet,
no eat wit' you hands.
Don't save me nothin',
it ain't in me plans.

I Mongoose Dentist,
just havin' me fun.
The varmints that came here
are all on the run.

Now they ain't smilin',
they's no teet' in they mout'.
No joke we makin',
the truth must come out.

———————————

Ted Torgersen

Flight of the Dangoose

The Devil throws a discus,
the Angel waits
on the ramp.
The day we know
is before us,
why don't we know why?

I escaped the land over me,
by flight.
I wasn't dealt with before,
or was the henhouse
wired for sound?

I left my life as a mongoose,
to escape the world of dentistry.
To you, in the All Star Joint,
it might sound like a mystery,
but we don't deal with that.

They saw him over to housing,
they saw him back to his kind.
Nobody knows the facts:
from what I can see he'd be
better off dead.

Don't fly: it could cost you.

There Is No Escape

A poet is like a mongoose,
playing stem to your stone,
branch to the breach
in the hull of your sensibilities;
acknowledging discord
where dissonance would do;
planting seedy harmonics
in a henhouse of delight,
the dentist his only nemesis,
pulling his words, like teeth,
with the pliers of oppression.

Wrong or right,
who is he
that writes all wrongs
in a litany of errors,
buried in the avalanche
of commerce?
Better to defy interpretation,
and slip quietly
into the enigma of chaos.

Whither away,
now that the curse is cast,
the gauntlet thrown,
your words, like teeth,
sown in pastures of plenty?
How does this simple silence
help you show a toothless
mongoose the way to steal eggs?

On the Way

I see mankind riding into
the twentieth century
on the back of a horse.
I watch him walk out again,
but I don't see who
carries the weight.

The War Horse can't carry it,
he too busy fightin' up.
Peace don't help him any,
he na drink from that cup.

Is there still a fountain,
that was not made
by the hands of men?

Why, do you think,
the mongoose steals eggs, man?
He tryin' to tell you somethin'!
Make you na hear?

Carry On

Carry you on,
carry you down,
the way, you don't believe it,
no mind see it.
It's already there,
so you are where you are;
no mind the preface, clown.

Mall redeem us, lord!
Already said, in other times;
to carry you while you were sleepin'?!
Was there anything else?!

The meeting at the henhouse
was purely by chance;
what do you think? (what)
It was all about? (chance??).
Redeem yourself: you don't need to…
Please yourself, after all.

Derive, downtown, never mind join.
Livin' in this country,
I came to your town.
I been in trouble since
I set my suitcase down.

Double the debt, so goes the pay.
C'est le guerre, pour le pay.
Glad I got me varmint suit.

CHAPTER FIVE:

The Wind and the Goats

The Wind and the Goats

Some days are so windy
that I wish some goats would come
and calm things down.

Ever see a goat on a windy day?
Something about them makes the wind stay away.
They are a force, like gravity,
that keeps the wind at bay.
Promising to blow tomorrow,
but staying calm today.

Maybe it's the way they smell,
so strong and, well, goatey,
that keeps the wind from trying
to ruffle their hair, knowing it'll never
get through all that powerful goatodor.
So it goes and blows itself away,
meaning to come back again some day
when there aren't so many goats in the way.

They are a force of nature, going not
so much toward something, or away, as *at* it.
Perhaps that's why they're called goats,
'cause they go *at*.
Have you ever seen many goats?
This country is really short on goats, I find,
just like it's short on poets.
Maybe it's a conspiracy
of Western archetypes,
cattlemen and sheep-men,
but no goat men, except one with balloons.
Maybe he borrowed their feet to keep the wind
from messing with his strings,
or maybe the goats are here, and no one notices.
Like no one can tell a poet, anywhere,
anytime, without a program,
and even then, can't tell him much.
Imagine John Wayne on the silver screen,
surrounded by a herd of goats, if you can.
History would really look different, then,
if anyone noticed.

Maybe then the weather channel
would use goats to predict wind patterns,
and we could all be lucky on the eights,
instead of the way we are now, without goats.
But the world's in no danger, no...
there are plenty of goats
in enough places to keep the wind at bay,
so the place don't just blow away
in a cross country goat race, except,
how do you keep them running?
Goats don't stampede, they exude, or recede,
going not away, but at, what they perceive.

It could be just a phase,
like childhood, or the hula-hoop,
and after years of struggle,
mankind could finally find itself
surrounded by goats,
becalmed on a hillside, far away
from the false winds
of changeable history.

Escape Goat

It was when the notice came,
addressed and sent in, in my name,
that I knew I had to make a goat change.

I made the most of what it said,
it was always there, in my head,
after all, they'll never know my name.
Just make it and be done,
and pretend it's all in fun.
I'm just goin' through a goat change.

Redemption is a fact,
somewhat like a sneak attack.
Now they say I'm comin' back,
just like a train without a track,
but it seems like another goat change.

They're countin' it up now,
but there's no way, no how,
that things will ever be the same.
Now they're skinnin' me,
and the most I could hope to be,
is a hide hangin' there for all to see.
So when you're chafin' at the bit,
just ease up on it,
we're goin' through another goat change.

It was nothing that he did,
when they were standing on the bridge,
he was tryin' to make a goat change.
Though I tried to rock the boat,
it seems it wouldn't float,
overloaded with the goat change.

Now the meat is fully fried,
I can see it in your eyes,
and they're still countin' up the goat change.
It's a caution to me,
like it was supposed to be,
'cause I'm livin' in a dream country.

I'm readin' and takin' note,
and they're countin' all the votes,
as they did away with hope,
but now they're goin' through a goat change.
The more things get rearranged,
the more they appear the same,
and though everyone's to blame,
we just gotta get past this goat change.

———————————

Alias, the Goatman

What the Cat-man do,
the Goat-man see.
Ain't neither one a them
better monkey with me,
that's right,
I'm gonna tell you a story tonight.

Nobody saw nothin'
'till they started to fight.
I didn't stay around for long,
it was a Saturday night,
that's right,
I had a better place to be that night.

A band was playin' rocksteady,
they didn't set up until late.
Cat-man won't say nothin',
said it's somethin' he ate.
Goat-man's story sounds a little fishy, too,
it won't come a new mornin'
until the night is through,
that's right,
everybody's got a story, tonight.

Cat-man was on the dance floor,
movin' left and right,
they partied in the hills somewhere,
it was a Saturday night.
Monkey seen it comin',
went an' hid out in the can,
what happened after that,
I just can't tell you, man.
That's right,
I'm tellin' you a story tonight.

Come Monday mornin',
there was nothin' left to say.
The cops and the ambulance
had all come and gone away.
Goat-man told his story,
lucky to be alive,
the song that I'm a singin'
is gonna show up all their lies.
That's right,
it was just another Saturday night.

———————————————

Where Are They Now?

"I am not yet ost",*
said the Cheesman,**
in deference to his name.
"I don't really see why
they call me that,
they know I'm not to blame."***

Coarse bread and onion,
he casts them aside,
and turns away his nose
for the sake of his pride,
which is inexorably tied
to the cattlemens' association....****

Meanwhile, back at the branch
of the ranch,*****
where the ranch branches off
into branches of ranches,
a foul wind arises,
with nothing to slow it down,
let alone stop it.

*Gjetost is a Scandinavian goat cheese that few people like.
**This ain't the one from Newaulkie, that's for sure.
***Blame is where you find it, mate.
****Railroads, mines and factories, incorporated.
*****Old it may be, it's noplace like home.

Game Over

Goats were once a part
of the reality we share,
now they're almost invisible,
and no one seems to care.

Windy days or calm,
they could be just a myth;
history is funny like that,
you never know how it is.

Why are sheep and cows
socially acceptable,
while the mere mention of goats
meets with disapproval?

They have horns, like the others do,
and there's a lot of nothing made
from that about what the devils do.
More goats would be better,
just to spread the blame;
but even if there weren't any,
things would be about the same.

The elephant still works,
just like the elevator,
only thing, there's no inspection permit,
go figger.

God 'ear what you say,
when you speak the truth,
and when you lie,
His sky is the roof.

The world's just a prison,
you cannot get away,
there's no place called home,
and nowhere else to stay.

———————

CHAPTER SIX

David Captain

Big Hill Revisited

The space suited florist's man
is dumping dead daisies
out the back of a blue van,
into the alley at dawn.

It begins like a journey,
a long day like any other,
so full, and filled in every detail,
making it clear at last,
demanding solidity, not dreams,
from a land empty of promise.

Like a missed step, fallen through
the cracks of a grassy sidewalk,
the big hill looms, indistinct,
backdrop for a land
merely noticed, not seen.

For a trip through here is like any other:
you need a suitcase and a trunk.
The trains run on time, a fossil fuel,
indeed, like trucks through the night,
relentless and unceasing.

Meanwhile, the fateful are tolled,
one by one, into another routine day
by the savory smells of soups
and almost forgotten stews,
in the late night and early
morning hours, that sustain them.

I am the traveler,
and I am the road.
On this morning
bright as dust,
leading out,
I follow myself
where no man goes,
anymore: Big Hill,
as if they ever did.

* * * *

The Two Signs:

Big Hill

Pop. 0 Elev. 0

HOTEL
CALIFORNIA

Ball lightening flickers around the signs,
as across the road, a spectral figure
takes shape from the swirling foxfire,
a crackling debacle for the senses,
as David Captain, for it is he,
looks to the East,
where the bloated, red sun rises,
and the figure speaks.

Ghost:

I am waiting
for the world
to wake up
and I am waiting
for a poet to come
who will make
the world safe,
at last,
for poetry,
thereby ending slavery,
and I am waiting
for the snows
of Kilimanjaro
to finally finish melting
so the seas can rise
and I am waiting
for the thunder
to split
in disguise,
and I am waiting
for the new morning
to finally dawn
in a rebirth of wonder.

David Captain:

Sir—
I thought you were…

Poet:

Dead?
What is death
but a change
of mind,
a memory
left behind
in a place
named "Here"
at the foot
of the mound
of buried seers,
no longer somewhere
in Arkansas.

David Captain:

But I was told…

Poet:

That I would
be waiting
as I said I was,
but for *you*?
Lies and promises,
empty
as the mouths
they issued from,
led you,
but where?
From there
to another nowhere,
just not
the same one.

David Captain:

Nowhere, but now here...

Poet:

And the several smokes
of their many fires
mingle with
the steam
from coffeepots
that the wind blows,
on a clear day,
back whence they came,
back, and back...

David Captain:

To Bait-il-Fakih!
The man of the desert
knew they must
someday return,
the monsoon
filling the sails
of their leaky dhows
to rimwrack at last
on that far burning shore.

Poet:

Ah!
So, you remember
something,
at least.
I thought...

David Captain:

That lingering
would belie me
this place,
ever fabled
by the daughters
of memory,
only to guile me out
of a place
that was never
meant to be home,
any more than
Big Hill was
meant to be Zion.
You know,
in all that time
I spent there,
I never knew
it's name.

Poet:

Jack Ford's!
A brave new world
if ever there was one,
and no way out
save the obvious,
and no one
ever took it,
'till now.

David Captain:

No one?
But I heard...
whispers, almost,
of others...

Poet:

A painter,
a saloonkeeper,
a philosopher
and two folksingers,
a carpenter
and a rock band
and a novelist,
a dancer
and an architect,
who had big plans
and still does,
for that matter.
What of them?
They left, but
not to pass
this way again.

David Captain:

So, there is another road, then?

Poet:

The show must
go on,
though it plays
to an empty house
in these hollow times.
They became
a latter day
company of minstrels,
pitching their tents
here one night
and there the next,
and were joined
by mountebanks
and jugglers
and an illusionist,
contortionists
geeks
and stuntmen,
in a cultural
renaissance,
a carnival
of real splendor.
But no one
knows where
they truly went.

David Captain:

Not even you, sir?

Poet:

The seed
of truth bears
bitter fruit at last.
If I lived
I could but
publish and perish,
which amounts
to the same thing,
back there.

David Captain:

Then what of me, now,
who am neither
published nor perished,
but sitting here in limbo
while the tides run,
springing and neaping
down the long seasons?

Poet:

You must
cry tough,
as you did
so long ago.
It never mattered
if anyone listened.
There are those
for whom
it is tough
to cry,
even as it is
for you.
But you
must cry tough
as you grow old,
for then no man
may take
your measure.
For it was written,
long ago:
man must be tough,
tougher than the world.

* * * *

The spectral fires blaze up,
then die, as two ravens,
their crackling cries
echoing one another,
first circle, then flap suddenly
toward the sinking sun,
the silver sheen
of their wings lighting
a path to that farther shore,
as yet undelineated,
that is the beginning
and end of all songs.

And now, our hero,
for whom Hell was created,
with solemn steps
and an empty heart,
begins the journey,
not of a lifetime,
but all eternity,
as the first clouds,
heavy with promise,
herald the hurricane breeze.

———————

Song of the Oppressor

In the country of the oppressor
only one idea is king:
do what I say,
and forget what it means to think.
Glittering concrete,
asphalt, steel, and glass;
pretend it has value,
and forget about the past.

Forget about singing,
forget all the songs,
might makes you right,
even when you are wrong.
See the sunset of culture
as tourism's song.*

* Personal feelings aside, this is it, folks.

The empty eyes
of the walking dead,
soulless, unfeeling,
the country of dread;
don't think about it,
everything is alright.
If you feel you need refuge,
just seek you Mother Night.*
Darkness means refuge,
yeah, you got it right.
Just remember what I told you:
might never makes right.**

In the land of the oppressor,
the watchword is fate, not faith.
Hear what I'm saying,
it's never too late.***
And all along,
the watchtowers
that were erected,
were not symbols
of a cultural Babylon,
after all.****

* Double trouble, and it don't show on the surface.
** Denial is the drug of choice here. See Marlowe's
Dr. Faustus: "Get thee behind me!," too late.
*** The poet speaks, but who hears?
**** Indeed!

I tried, but now I'm tired,
it's clarity I seek.
In the country of the oppressor,
there's no one left to meet.
Close all the windows,
and bar all the doors,
push all the buttons,
and then light the fuse.
The new morning
ain't coming,
it just has to refuse.*

It's a done deal**
as desert covers the world,***
moral and mortal,
for your untolled elucidation:
see what I mean.
As you grow older,
the packages things come in
get harder and harder to open,
in the land of the oppressor.
Why is that?

* Recidivism as an analogy for the human condition.
** De'il in Scottish dialect, deil' to some.
*** World as veldt und verstellung.

Anansi, the spider,
walked out one morning
and up the waterspout.
Daphne Duck,
not Dikki, worse luck,
says, singing:*
"It's only me,
only me;
I want you
to remember
only me."**
Oh, well, try again.***

I remember the oppressor
in verse and in song,
you're probably still wondering
what took me so long.
Ideas are mighty:
they curb them
though we scream.
We culture is a threat to them,
it's not what it seems.****

* Yes, but "Tonight's the Night."
** Not an ordinary washout, but a deluge.
*** Ok for a spider, too bad you're outta time, dude.
**** Another tourist attraction.

In the country of the oppressor,
the hammer is down.
Hit the nail on the head,
and never made a sound.
This isn't news, no,
it ain't nothing new;
besides, all we can hear
is the turning of the screw.*
South, the legend says,
is a land free from strife.
A roots man could go there,
and start a new life.**

In the land of the oppressor
they're dealin' dope,
dealin' guns.
I don't ask why they do it,
I assume it's for fun.***
In the land of the oppressor,
a happy man can't sing.
He sees what the birds see,
but he can't do a thing.****

* Nails for your coffin, screws if you like, pie a la mode is nothing like life.
** Squatters need not apply.
*** Got nothin' better to do, Breds.
**** Only he knows why.

In the land of the oppressor,
you give the de'il his due.
You know what lies sound like,
and crave what is true.
They say they'll rule forever,
until the trumpets call,
forever, until that fateful day,
when Babylon must fall.*
Clearly, that can never happen
in the land of the oppressor,
where even the truth is a lie.**

* * * *

* They sing a song here that goes like this: "You and me, you and me,
today and then tomorrow, there's only me, only me."
** Currently held aloft by balloons filled with a trick gas.

Dramatis Personae:

David Captain: poet and wanderer.
Deal: a gambler.
Traveler in Black: courtesy of John Brunner.
Daisy Jane: a goat (deceased).

* * * *

Hunger did not draw him,
he felt no abiding thirst.
I would like to say that
in his indeterminate wandering,
he ate dates from the calendar,
and the sand, which is there,
at last, on that farther shore,
but he did not reach it.
Instead, with foresight,
he packed a road salad,
and absorbed its very essence
into his being,
and it was sufficient.

So he walked a crooked path,
and he walked for many a mile,
and he came at last to a low hill,
and he walked with a certain style.
Indistinct, at first, it appeared
like any other bald knob,
but then he saw it was a midden,
that glowed with the opalescence
of shells blackened with age,
whose light was at first diffused,
then absorbed,
by the figure of a man in black,
who held a crooked staff;
and he spoke for the first time
since leaving history.

David Captain:

So?!

Traveler in Black:

You have come,
as I knew you must,
with caution to the winds
of a hurricane past.
Did it seem a long time to you?

David Captain:

What is time,
but the simplest of things,
that hurries one on,
like two raven's wings?

Traveler in Black:

Not three, as is my custom,
but only one shall I grant;
that which is in your mind,
and not your heart.

David Captain:

How did you know?
I have not spoken to anyone.

Traveler in Black:

By the ravens at your shoulder
it is written and read.
I grant you one wish,
though you'd be better off dead.
As you wish, so shall you see,
and what you see,
so shall it be.

And with that, he turned
and disappeared into the bald hill,
trailing his cloak behind him,
like a legacy of endless pain.

* * * *

Deal:

If a hen and a half
can lay an egg and a half
in a day and a half,
how long would it take a man
to sandpaper an elephant
down to the size of a bulldog?*

* Half a man, way I see it.

David Captain emerges,
as if from a dream,
to find himself on a platform,
waiting for a train.*
He hears his own heart beating,
like a pendulum swingin' on a chain.
The gambler approaches him,
a deck of cards in his hand,
offering a cut.
David Captain declines,
and the gambler cuts to the Queen of Spades,
but the cards are all the same.
It is then that David Captain
notices the curly hairs
sprouting from the man's palm,
and resolves not to shake his hand.

Deal:

All aboard, that train, all aboard.
The Ares Bethlehem Railroad proudly presents
From Here to Eternity
and a free bottle of castile soap
to each of the faithful,
all on one train.
Don't need no ticket,
you just get on board.

* Not the one named *The City of New Orleans*, that's for sure.

David Captain:

> I see they've changed the name
> of this ordinary looking town
> to Desolation Road,
> or is that just the station?

Deal:

> It's only one town,
> one stop on the road to glory.
> It'll be here soon,
> I can hear the rails a hummin':
> it don't matter if the sun don't shine, no,
> it's all right,
> we're goin' to the end of the line.
>
> David Captain is silent,
> as he surveys the dead town,
> the empty buildings,
> the blue florist's van,
> tires rotted to the rims,
> behind which stands a spectral goat,
> eating a bunch of dry, dead flowers.

Daisy Jane:

> Let him go,
> even if he complains,
> just don't you
> go getting' on that train,
> 'cause it ain't goin' nowhere.*

* And you've already *been* there.

Deal:

> Don't pay that ghost goat any mind.
> She choked to death on some
> hippy candy bar* she found,
> 'long about the time
> the town up and died.

Daisy Jane:

> He's all this town ever was,
> and sure it ain't no lie:
> the truth lived and died here,
> on the Fourth of July.
> That's why no one's left,
> they were all his slaves,
> and I'm just a ghost of a goat,
> that'll haunt him across the age.**

Deal:

> Step right up, Capt'n, sir,
> the train's right before your eyes.
> Don't listen to that pesky goat,
> she's the devil in disguise.***

*A Wha Guru Chew. New Age soul food.
** Goat as devil's conscience: the horns of a dilemma, indeed.
*** Scapegoat, yes, but there is no escape.

Daisy Jane:

> This song has no beginning,
> it neither has an end.
> You meet yourself in memories,
> that cause your mind to bend.
> Don't get on that gleaming train,
> let it go on down the track.
> It's a long and lonely way, from here,
> and there ain't no coming back.*

*   * * * *

> The rails just kept on hummin',
> after the train was outta sight,
> the sky was partly cloudy,
> it might be morning,
> it could be night.
> And David Captain wandered silently,
> into the uncertain light,
> for he had fallen out
> of the habit of speaking.

Deal:

> Step right up here, folks,
> this train's bound for glory.
> Don't miss your only chance,
> at all that's holy.

* They never tell you that when you buy your ticket.

Daisy Jane:

> Fulla holes,* more like.
> Try as he might,
> he could never get it right.
> This town's not even a memory,
> it all happened in one night.
> But there's other towns like this one,
> and they ain't home,** either.

David Captain:

> The world is as it ever was,
> the way we saw it first.
> But this doesn't satisfy my hunger,
> or begin to slake my thirst.

* * * *

> Now, eternal wanderer,
> have your passport ready,
> for no matter how far you roam,
> there is no place called home.
> That train has left the station,
> with two lights on behind.
> The blue light is your sorrow,
> and the red light is for all time.
> The town that the oppressor built,
> that stifled all your songs,
> appeared, at first, a sanctuary,
> but even that was wrong.

---

* Or Fuller brushes.
** Not a new concept for the human heart.

CHAPTER SEVEN:

The Soap Mills of France

The Soap Mills of France

Bring me soap and coffee,
and a picture of Khadafy,
sitting in the evening,
listening to the wind blow.

Don't try to suppress me,
or even second guess me,
I'm as lonely as a soldier
in a war where nobody cares.

Keep track of the time,
and organize your mind,
there's no reason to seek
that you can find.

But the soap and the coffee
will keep me up talkin'
nonsense for the rest of the night.
And the races I've run in
weren't for fun and
I don't want to do it again.

So bring soap and coffee,
and I won't look behind me,
on my way to the Soap Mills of France,
'cause ain't nobody lookin' for me.

Eclipse

They said, "Something is coming."
And asked, "Boy, a where you go?"
Me say, "I gone Tegucigalpa
for a meeting with Fidel Castro."
He se'f didn't show,
so me gone home
to a land filled with sorrow
and built up a scarecrow.

Now, if a father lies,
his children can know the truth.
And if anybody should cuss them,
they mark themselves uncouth.
To prevent all this from happening,
the way, it's nothing new:
just tell them
"they ass business,"
and go on with what you do.

A man there out a road,
is a studyin' the moon.
Like it have a face carved there,
that a go away very soon.
When he come back, now,
this question me a ask:
"Now that you see he face, again,
did little while you see he back?"

"No, the world didn't make so,"
said a voice from on high.
"You only see the moon face to face
when he is in disguise."
So, now you have the answer,
it's written oh so clear:
when the sun is shining bright,
the moon just isn't here.

———————

Doctor Doom's Car Wash

At Dillon's grocery,
where we sat we se'f down,
it's a cool place for limin'
when everybody's around.
It now name Doctor Doom Car Wash,
let me tell you why.
Doctor Doom, he a come there,
and he try an' he try.

He a wash a' them car,
twenty dollar he charge,
late into the evening,
he workin' so hard.
'Long as the shop open,
and even after he close,
Doctor Doom a wash car there,
and wet up we clothes.

Use Your Fingers

Set the cart before the man,
and watch everything go wrong.
Set it before the horse,
at the time they sound the gong.

You better get yourself goin'
according to the sound,
that ain't a game they're playin',
like you hear talk about in town.

The appointed manager is an onion,
but we suspected that all along.
Why is it you don't like the smell,
'cause of something that you done?

Do it like I told you,
do it when the morning comes,
it's up to you to put it together,
we picked you 'cause you're all thumbs.

———————————

Look Homeward, Now

Lead me home, now,
like a horse to water,
or a lamb to slaughter;
like a goat on display,
with his head on a plate
and the rest of him
artfully draped on a hatrack
in the window of the abattoir.
Or like a pig's head on a stake,
eyes open wide,
lord of all he surveys.

Astray was a horse
that I attempted to ride,
and wherever he carried me
there was no place to hide.
Like a drunken sailor,
too free with his coign,
spendthrift like the wind,
washed away with the tide,
like a castle built of sand
and crumbled with pride.

———————

House of Cards

They built up a house, made out of cards,
that they dealt from a pack of lies.
It's the reason for these desperate times,
and nobody is acting surprised.

The Tower is called *I Told You So,*
with a parapet all around,
they didn't bother building a fire escape,
so there's no other way to get down.

They called the place *Lord Have Mercy,*
and with it claimed a place in the sun.
Now all of the people who let it fall down,
say they're sorry for what they have done.

Sorry for what they have done, have done,
and they say it, each and every one;
they look for somebody to pick up the pieces,
while they wait for the morning to come.

I say there's still time,
while they're standing in line,
to deal the cards all over again.
Yes, gather them up and deal a new hand,
before the game finally comes to an end.

It would be payment in kind,
at the end of the line,
to see them buried alive,
ass deep in their lies,
and promises never received.

Brain Drain

The rain is gently fallin', an'
it's fillin' up the ditch,
runnin' quickly down the drain.
The water that is in the gutter,
was used to wash your brain.

Call me back when you feel better,
make it, like, tomorrow night.
Since there's nothing left on your mind,
can you finally see the light?

The country needs more comfort,
and the city has too much crime.
It's all so damn faceless,
and there's nowhere left to hide.

Even on a stormy night,
with the stars all safely hidden,
it's like the lives we all once lived
were wasted doing as we were bidden.

Find a way to free yourself,
and no longer be a puppet or a slave.
If there is no other way,
let freedom at last lie with you
in a sodden grave.

Pet Monkey

Sometimes the words never change,
like the sound of the rain,
that beats out a rhythm
on the roof.

People and places change,
they even change their names,
but what they say always sounds the same:
"Come here, boy, if you wanna
pet my monkey."

The first thing she said to me,
was that nobody rides for free,
at least not if the circus
is in town.

So the rain keeps fallin' down,
and there's water on the ground,
that's never stoppin'
on it's way to the sea.

It just common courtesy,
but something you rarely see,
to reply, "That wasn't me,
I'm afraid that your monkey might bite."

And so on through the night,
in the rain and dim light,
by the river, on it's way to the sea,
you'll have to pardon me,
I just wanted to be free,
and not have to pay to see your monkey.
No, I don't wanna pay to pet your monkey.
Times like this I can't complain,
listenin' to the rain,
and the song that it plays, upstairs.
And it's easy enough to see,
there's no reason to bother me,
'cause you got a monkey, and nobody cares.

Now, in the light of day
the rain has gone away,
and last night is nothin' but a dream.
Newspaper headlines scream
that the circus has been washed clean,
but nobody has seen your monkey.

Pass It Over

Every day, in the morning,
a truck, it does pass,
and carry 'way everything
to the labas.
The fruits of our labors,
gone from we at last,
some to the post office,
the rest with the trash.

No one can know
what tomorrow may bring,
so call upon the living
with the song that you sing.
Try for understanding,
it's not easy, not free,
but if a entertainment you come for,
better listen to me.

Just you pass it over,
before you go 'long.
It's a feeling with a rhythm
that you're hearin' so strong.
Go on, pass it over,
It's only a song:
if you bring it and sing it,
you'll never go wrong.

Politics

In this district,
there was a piece of cheese,
the devil,
and a loaf of bread.
How does a sane man
make a choice like that?

Ain't no choice for me,
you see, daylight come
and me want for go home.
Yes, dayclean a come
and me want to go home.

Yeah, man, you can talley me load.
I told you what I told you,
and now I gone down the road
with a bottle of no corrode.

And that's the end of the episode,
as if you didn't know,
when you gave them the code,
and wrote what you knew they would have said,
if they had any freedom at all.

———————————————

Look Behind You, Now*

The dust of today
will be your window on tomorrow,
and when the dust is dust,
whither away, Mystery Babylon?

I ain't talkin' 'bout geology, no,
the mystery lies elsewhere,
in case you can't see,
the answer is in geophagy.

Yes, eat a peck of dirt,
and then you can die.
Does it matter where it comes from?
It's right before your eyes.

Come questions, come answers,
come you, with all your lies.
Nobody is even here
that will make a reply.

Mystery Babylon, may he ever rest,
in his own personal Zion,
and to Hell with the Joker,
he did it all in jest.

* For Ivanhoe Martin.
Just a fool in cheap clothing
put paid to the rest.
There's no bird surfer sitting
in your Babylon nest.

The migration of the mighty
long ago, was foretold.
They're leavin' this world
because your hearts are so cold.

Those of we who are rhygin
don't often last long,
we're the voice of your conscience,
in legend and song.

We say there's more to this life
than doin' what you're told,
and for we the worst punishment
is to ever grow old.

I Remember Arnold

I remember Arnold,
as if it were yesterday.
But it's only a reflection,
that will not go away.

Acting like he used to act,
movement without pause;
as quietly he rode in,
and out on another horse.

I remembered Arnold,
and forgot about the cost;
and if I saw him
on the street today,
I'd tell him to get lost.

I remember Arnold,
I wish not quite as well;
I wish that he
would forget 'bout me,
and go on straight to Hell.

Don't pay no mind
to the preacher,
just make you mark him well:
at the slack,
the waters cross,
and listen for the bells.

—————————

Elevator

I went down to the music shop,
they've got an elevator
that does not stop.
I rode that 'vator
to the second floor,
son of a bitch,
I couldn't open the door.

(chorus)

Said a moe ni moe
an' a moe ni moe,
an' a moe ni moe no mo'.
I tried and tried,
but I couldn't get out.
Won't someone please tell me
what it's all about?
It kept on goin'
right to the top,
maybe somebody should
call the cops.

(chorus)

I saw an old man
sittin' on the roof.
I said, "Please, mister,
tell me the truth."
He said, "Do what you want,
I don't care,
but you'll live a lot longer
if you take the stairs."

(chorus)

One Love

Age promises endless pain,
to balance youth's fruitless strife.
Many walkers went out walking,
and the talkers kept on talking,
been chowderheads all they life.

Memory, like a frozen stain,
abrupt as ever,
stops thought's bulbs from sprouting
in a winter landscape of the mind,
still, as never before.

Strike up, ye band members,
and play soft and low,
for 'tis alla we
beyond the sunset must go,
and relive the story
from those lost days of glory,
where we once walked
through life hand in hand.

Catch Me If You Can
Watch words,
with finality,
make statements
of gravity,
like the present,
never mind,
like the past.

See the end of
something new,
then watch out
what you do,
gravity will bring
you down here,
at last.

Oceans of mystery,
like the pages
of history,
won't say
why we hid
'fore the mast.

Find something new,
and see,
the morning through,
that the dice,
they are already cast.

———————

New Day

Morning will come
to the place
where I stay,
and it will bring
with it,
when it comes,
a new day;
yes, hear me when I say,
there will come another day,
it will bring us
another new day.

As I watch the firelight,
through the long,
long winter's night,
foreday morning
will come to me,
I say.
Where I sit,
by the fireside,
at peace,
because I tried;
to stop waiting
for the dawning
new day,
a new day.

New day, new day,
it will come and be today,
and bring the renewing light
of the sun,
yes, the sun.

Now, the night is nearly passed,
and the firelight will be surpassed,
by the dawning glory
of the new day,
a new day.

In this morning,
I will stay,
I, man, to listen and to pray,
that it's gonna be
a brand new day.
Man, I living for another
new day,
a new day.

Another day,
another day,
more like those
that have gone away,
a new day,
yes I say,
one more day.
I will live again,
this day,
and once again,
hear me say,
it's gonna be
a brand new day.

———————————

Go to the Devil!

God said "I only take Devil Weed,
in exchange for forgiveness,
or whatever you want.
Din't they tell you that
back there, where you started out?"

I was already in a bad way
when I heard this;
more than I'm doing,
I don't want to deal with.
Why don't you leave me alone?

Condemn me for what I didn't do,
make it easy for the rest of them
to finally get through.
Go on, and do right by you.

I'm already past the roundup,
and finally, the train has left the station,
I can still taste the coffee that remains in the cup,
but it's not really cause for celebration.

———————————

Might, They Find, and the Definitions

Wait until April's over,
before you March into May.
The season is the reason
for the way it is every day.

Wait upon the devil's district,
that you paid for, yourself.
Try to make it mean something,
besides what's waiting on the shelf.

Time is waiting for you,
or someone else that it left behind.
It's like walkin' through an open country,
pretending to be blind.

Don't look where you were told to look,
you won't see what you can't find.
Cook what there is to cook,
what's on your mind is so simple,
more than half the time.

Dig a little deeper,
to the layer of buried truth.
Work is not beneath you, yet,
wait until you're on the roof.

I am the dorty mind,
and I am the door you must pass under.
Do yourself a favor, and never go there,
even just for a look.

Time was once such a mighty thing,
with endlessness at its beck and call.
A horse is what got you here,
is there any way out at all?

There is always a way out,
but you might not recognize the path.
Something you fail to notice
will make you wait until it's too late.

Are you one of those who is waiting on the war?
Is that why nothing is on your mind
that wasn't there before?
Or was it that you were made another way,
and sought refuge from all this sordid foolishness?

This is the time, and you should make the most of it,
don't waste your days like I did, in regret.
There will be time enough for that
when you find out what it all meant.

You must be getting tired
of this radio station, by now,
playing the same song over and over,
like nothing could ever go wrong;
but that's the way it will be,
'till the lights finally go out,
and the curtain comes down.

Dirt

I am called dirt,
and man, I'm diggin' it.
The worse you think of me,
the more there is, you see,
until the end,
and dirt's endless, man,
like I told you.

I am the time
and time is running out on you.
The sands that slip away, unnoticed,
are not solid, like dirt.
The shifting sands that
keep track of time can run out.
They're makin' their great escape now,
too bad no one is paying attention.
Better look while you still can.

Migration

We've all lost our way
at one time or another,
and that is why we watch birds.
They always know
when it's time to migrate.
There is nothing for them to fear,
when the time to move on draws near,
there is nothing that the birds haven't heard.

A yellowtail on a wall,
or a hummingbird near the fence,
they know when the time has come.
The aline singing in the shadows
can't say where they've gone.
It's a different country,
one that you've never seen;
even if you manage to get there,
you won't know what it means.
At least, to them,
they're not tourists, you see.
Birds live each day where they are,
wherever that happens to be.

That could also be you,
it could even be me,
cross over, for a minute,
to an open country.
A mile is a minute
of your life's journey gone by.
Make you open up your eyes
and see the reason why
we all need to migrate,
from time to time.
From ignorance, we need respite,
from oppression to take flight;
we need to turn day
into freedom from night.
Approximation can't save you,
like you once thought,
it's this haphazard thinking
which makes you get caught.

In this district, you can see,
it's starting to happen again,
and when it comes to migration,
now is better than when,
ever since the oppressor is making
everyone change their skin.
Like, if you don't do it,
think of the trouble you'll be in.
Better to fly far and fly fast,
than, in a season of darkness,
to breathe out your last.

There are some places, however,
where many people fear mice,
myself among them.
How do you differentiate
between fears like this?
Is there a way you can know
where you must go?
Can you migrate to a place
free from mice?

Would it be so much nicer there,
with nothing to fear, at the end,
but the mindless, nameless insects
that live in the bush?
Whether, by instinct or instigation,
or to establish a pattern
that we can understand,
the need to migrate stands foremost,
uniting heart and mind
in a desire to leave winter behind,
and like a shooting star, slip away,
to dance with the nightingale,
knowing that the journey stops with you.
Waste Your Time

I pissed my life into
the district of your wastebasket.
I din't do it 'cause I wanted to,
and I tried hard to resist.

The faster they go into your
passing lane of life,
the more they need to slow down
and listen to this, my story.

Talk is cheap, and so is life,
ask me why I told you this,
there wasn't any reason,
except for the strife,

that encompasses your life,
don't think about it twice,
more of the meaning will come with time,
and it won't be all that nice.

In the valley that is behind,
you can't see, nor do you want to.
In the alley of your mind,
it's according to what you see through,
that makes you seek and find.

Reality is just a word to which
they give too much play,
if you heard what I told you here,
there'd be nothing left to say.

The Human Telephone

They say all men are liars,
and that's why they can't live alone.
I see myself as a telephone,
that's my line,
but if I had any sense,
I'd change into a cafeteria,
and liquefy the good green grease of intent
into a pea soup for the masses,
and allow talking only at mealtimes.

This is my message to you…
There's really nothing to worry about
as long as someone else
pays the bill.

———————————

Mystery Upon Mystery

It's like living in a land far away,
where pretend battle axes
are trying to do battle,
and almost cattlemen
are attempting to herd cattle.
Mankind makes his war noises,
and acts like he's addled,
and it's always the same, every day.

You can't try to wish it away.
It wouldn't mean anything,
or work, any way,
so, dry all your tears, I say.

I wanted to find me a place,
along the American roadside,
a place to peacefully abide,
where I could finally hide
from all the excess and pride,
and then go on a bolo hunt.

———————————

Every Motion Counts

The dismal, destructive Newstand,
doing it's utmost,
still cannot undo
the least of all
the things, that the thing
we do does do.

Wake up and live,
deny yourself the doubt,
that's why the way you came to be
was likely so round about.

Cross all the rivers,
don't even begin to count
the burnt bridges.
The rivers all run at the same time,
and there's really no way out.

Go into motion, now,
and make yourself count.
Don't worry about those
for whom the thing that matters,
is only the amount.

Tell them this story, do not lie,
they have to hear about it, bye and bye.
Say what is on your mind,
if you don't leave nothin' out,
they can't waste your time
pretending not to know
what this is all about.

Ted Torgersen

Afterword: Workin Progerse

Tell me, skip, so what's it gonna be then, eh? She issued the K. M. R. I. A. in fine fashion, twice, no less, like a true Sister of Charity, a fine Christian bastion, upholder of all the faith, without hope, without end, for her namesake, allmen. And became, the morecome, the song of which it brings, and the seasons of the heart in the evening are always her own. What do you want me to do, to see if it's true? Like an ancient prophet, estimated, Rain-in-the-Box, to assuage the Pain-in-Life, words unclear, to the foremast of Holds-Himself-Up, where no man comes, old after elder, hold until older, in moremansland they came without her and brought a vicious return to night's awning. A true slam dunk. And now, in the glittering twilight of our times, we see ourselves, again, against the wicket, stumping our bandwagon once more throughout history on the three legs of man. Over the hump and down the dale, we're traveling many a mile to keep from getting hung from the gallows of our own intentions and lackluster inventions. Time, and time alone will tell, think you're in Heaven, but you're livin' in Hell.

Nor am I out of it. I'm near to the wall, and he's out in the hall, and there's no sense to it at all. Mutter's no matter, I'm mad as a hatter, and won't answer questions or calls. More costly, as said by our own forestory shortener, with wrath in his mines, as a factory girl, dressed to the nines, with more goop than gander, under a pillbox hat, reminded us to note that the boat wouldn't float, farely, you mowat, underseadiving, amongst all the fishes, that seem so delicious, to those with nothing but teeth in their mouths. So the story gets shorter, the longer we wait, the days are like daisies, blooming too late, and the miles add up, no more than they must, 'cause after them comes the long rest in the dust.

As he Elbowed his way, Parsely, past us without a word, cryin' all the time, like a hound dog, the same old story every time, it's the only one he knows: like the morning sun it comes, and like the wind it goes. Fate rien round the maypole, where fortunes are found, not made, like the purple maze you're running, through life's long lost loves and leaves, like loaves and misses, bread upon the waters, not the oil that I want, viscous and nasty seeming, under the midnight moon. More to be pointless, undoubtedly that was your question, what is the meaning of this? Once, I looked at both sides, now, but still, somehow, it left me bested by my illusions, in a quandary, like running the same race twice, for the third charm, like a sheep on a shingle, trying to mingle, where there's no room for improvement, let alone anyone else. And, for a fuse scents, bought bothofthem's hatchet, exchanged for a packet, and got a sense of change for a penny, earned, and that's as much as we've learned at the back of the fish truck, so help me load.

They told me to tell you all of this quickly, now, 'cause there's a Hellhound on my trail, where the night winds wail, and shelter from thishitstorm of who said it's his story, where it's safe and warm, is more construction than mystery, after all. That was last night. Tonight, as the song goes, we have a really big show planned for all you folks in the permanent gallery, an onlooker's paradise, please have your tickets ready and mind your boots, goin' up. Ah, what tangled webs we weave, for after we are weevils, they baked in we bread, like our fathers before us once said, when they told you so. A really big show.

Start fisk and Finnish after, no balkin', you quackers, the sky's in your eye like a big pizza pie, with ducks the limit, in his owen wordsworth, like a cry in the willow mist, neveremembering where it all started. Came to sit, at most half hearted, and broke wind to your sails, enough for a new horizon, like the song said, over the hills and far away, it's not a place you stay, it's a state of mind, you say, the true home of the human heart. That's enough cheers for your wirehouse, I've got a tent to rent.

More to the point, the fabric of the universe includes all that we know, all we want to know, everything we can speculate about, and on top of it all, whatever else that we cannot even begin to imagine. In the midst of all this are the songs, the prime entelechy, the intrinsic harmonic energies that cause the universe to constantly renew and re-invent itself. That is why the quest for internal harmonics within a language is mankind's highest endeavor, for the songs find their way into our thoughts and perceptions through the collective unconscious, and serve to maintain the internal harmonic balance of creation in our daily lives. No language me a language, a talk me a talk.

Yes, and it has already been written what our world as we know it and dreamed if and made it, has become: "in the ignorance that implies impression that knits knowledge that finds the nameform that whets the wits that convey contacts that sweeten sensation that drives desire that adheres to attachment that dogs death that bitches birth that entails the ensuance of existentiality."* And after it is over, and we are dust, and even the dust is dust, who shall count the stars? Not me, for it is my fate to count the empty spaces between them. For alla we are stars that light the night, and emptiness is not just our reality, but our fate, whorled without end, at the edge the light bends, at the end of the night, allmen: the rest is silence.

July, 2010
* *Finnegans Wake* James Joyce, p. 18.

Fallen Empire

and Other Writings

Introduction

In writing the introduction to this, my second book, I find myself at a loss as to where to begin. To say that this is my final attempt at literature, made at the end of a largely wasted and useless life, is insufficient to convey the sense of frustration and loss that I feel at this writing.

All attempts to publish *Out of Exile* have been fruitless, and although some people were sympathetic, no one was convinced that it was worth the effort to defy an act of oppression that spanned five decades when the object of it would be dead in a few years, anyway. Better to let complacency rule than to derail the freight train of the oppressor. My dream of making a living as a writer died long ago, and I present this work, as I did the last one, for literary purposes only.

A note on the text: these poems and the two prose pieces were written between 2010 and the present with two exceptions. Both *Wait for the West Wind* and the lyric *Who Am I* were written on the same day in the fall of 1968 and submitted anonymously through a fellow student to prevent their being stolen or suppressed. *Wait for the West Wind* appeared in New Yorker magazine and elsewhere, author unknown, and the lyric *Who Am I* was recorded and copy written by Country Joe and the Fish. I have no provenance for either, but have included them because they are mine and represent my best work.

The Ivory Towers of Babylon and *West Indies in Transition: Bay to Guest House* were written for a West Indian audience, and the latter piece is written in the dialect spoken there. Another version may have appeared in a local magazine by a different author, but this is my version of what was discussed. *The Ivory Towers of Babylon* also may have appeared with the byline Ivanhoe Martin, a Jamaican folk hero who died in the nineteen forties, and who provided the prototype for the character Rhygin in the 1970s movie *The Harder They Come*, starring Jimmy Cliff. (See *Out of Exile*, chapter 1).

The poem *Fallen Empire* is my latest and longest effort and segues the *David Captain* chapter in *Out of Exile*, although the main character is conspicuously absent. If you like, you may see him as the author's persona, doing a penance by writing a poem that likely no one will ever read. The torch has been passed, but, alas, the fire is out. I have now combined the two works into one volume and plan to self publish.

September 2014

Fallen Empire

Fallen Empire

Across the universe,
since the beginning of time
lies the curse of Babylon,
an extremity of crime.

Of course, it's so easy
to forgive or forget;
to remember is a challenge
to your humanity, if you still get.

All around the world,
in these here easy times,
it's the lotus of forgetfulness
that makes the truth fail to remind.

Gone again, gone again,
without hope to the end,
a reminder of mortality
is a truth that can't bend.

It's not about when,
and it's not even about now;
it's if you can catch me,
but it's not about how.

Gone are the days when it all seemed to work.
It's just an empty place now,
where you can't even buy a shirt,
or anything else that's of worth.

Is the devil wise
because he is old,
or because he is the devil?
Could this be why you don't understand?

Try to remember, it's not just a request.
Does this mean that it's too late
to resist the fickle
snare drum of fate?

Fallen Empire, not yet expired,
yet indeed dust, the harrow's too narrow
to do what you must:
to plow these endless fields free of rust.

Fallen Empire, system of oppression,
you are the absence of light,
the heart of darkness, the sufferer's plight.
Nothing exceeds like your excess.

Fallen Empire, surfeit of intention,
your minions are legion
but your name's never mentioned,
save by those who curse you.

I will kill you where you stand,
I will slay you in the shadow,
I will pave the way with your bones,
but only to show you the way home.
The fallen empire must die the death
that was wished upon me,
so that it's empty soul
may know redemption at last.

* * * *

For the fallen empire, indeedust, as we say, had an impecunious beginning, from the first thing to the last fast. Don't mistake the prose that you have proscribed, it is your undoing. Hear now! This is just the beginning! Across the universe they are discussing treason and greed, greed and treason, as if they were the same thing. Here, in the Fallen Empire, people never question anything, lest someone might hear. But still, when it finish falling it go lie right there. Empire.

Erase the erection of literary aspirations,
descend into the exile of extirpation,
as the fallen empire surrounds me now,
displaying it's ignorance, like a sacred cow.

Force yourself enough to see that
this song is a cry in the wilderness,
now that even the workplace is in distress,
for the Empire has fallen.

Strange beans grow in the desert of the fallen empire, but they are bound to expire without what is required to sustain life, even mental life, after humanity has departed. This is what your nation without culture did to me. When it affirmed treason it made me a man without a country. I only hope I have made this plain to you now, I been trying to tell you this for a long time, for awhile, now. It never seems to reach anybody who understands, somehow. Guess you wish you never read this, ent?

Fallen Empire, you are dust
in my hand forever,
and in this brave new world of no return
I will cry you a red river.

Fallen Empire, march along
until you realize you march alone.
As it was in the beginning
so it was all day long: fallen empire.

In this country of the blind
it's a one eyed song I sing,
where they bake the bread of sorrow
so that Rakon could be named king.

To get what you want in this life it must cost you,
but it's bound to cost someone else too.
So when you climb on the haycart be careful,
for it is then that your ass is gonna show.

In order to resist the oppressor,
you must understand what is crucial,
so that when you know you livin' in Babylon,
it is then you can stand up and be counted.

* * * *

Since philosophy is just a matter of consolidating ignorance, a society devoid of it must by definition be enlightened, but in reality things are not that simple, the dialectics of logic notwithstanding. Are we, the intelligentsia, invisible because no one can see us, or is it that we cannot even see ourselves because we have ceased to exist? Conundrums cause consternation, and riddles are meant to be solved; if this is true then why is life so hopeless, no matter how high the sky above?

In the life of grime there are five components: dust, soil, grease, dirt and dander. The seven causes of grime are more crucial, and define life in the Fallen Empire. There is grime caused by neglect, which is a way of life here. There is grime caused by squalor and slovenliness, one only has to observe the great lumpen proletariat to see a pattern of diminishing return. Grime is also caused by industrial activity, the price of progress, if you will. A'we so movin' up, or so it seems. Then there is cause number four, grime caused by the forces of nature such as dust storms, flood waters, wildfire and seismic activity. These are inexorable. Grime is also caused by malicious, willful or carelessly disrespectful activities that leave hair on the walls. Grime, however, is most often caused by the abovementioned five causes. This is the sixth cause. Lastly, there is the grime caused by natural attrition, that is, the crumbling of things with age and repeated use, the process by which things wear out and fall apart. Also, sometimes artifacts are defective and fall apart without providing any usefulness at all. It is as if modern life is one long unanswered prayer. Cast your bread upon the waters and find it after many days: soggy, scarcely edible and nibbled by tadpoles, carp and ducks, or scavenged by seagulls as the case may be. Prose writer in exile, poet no longer, trying to set things write at the edge of the abyss: vast emptiness, no holiness; another day in the same shirt. Whatever do you think might have been missed? Has the empire fallen while no one was looking, or is their worst yet to come? One thing is certain, Question Mark and the Mysterians aren't playing in the background, anymore. The time has come to smell the coffee brewed with 96 tears and either dunk your donut or take your place among the complacent, who have made all this possible. The choice is yours in the Fallen Empire.

The Empire of Babylon is fallen,
indeed dust. You may disagree
with what I told you,
but hear me, you must.
It's an evil mixture
of the blood and the dust,
where the vampire system
has finally gone to rest.

Babies were sacrificed
on the altar of greed,
women were desecrated,
whole lives went unlived.

When they reckon the fortune
that lay piled up in the shadows,
they first must walk the road they paved
with our bones and tarred with the marrow.

So the fortunes of war
coupled with the serenity of hate,
cost the whole world it's exemption
from the dictates of fate.

Fallen Empire, so long without standing,
not to be remembered for a day or an evening
in this long afternoon on Earth,
not even worth mentioning.

Fallen Empire, can you now see the ending,
a fallen empire with nothing left standing.
Are you almost contrite,
will that see you through the night,
or will there be a new day based on understanding?

When your minions are dust,
along with all of their works,
may you never be excused for the
humanity that was denied by your existence.

Gone away, gone away
like the songs of yesterday,
swallowed with the tears of today,
echoed in the new morning of reason resounding.

Going out singing is not always as easy
as walking alone in the rain.
You only have to ask the Poet in Exile,
but don't expect him to explain.

All that awaits you, now,
is oblivion, the final frontier,
and all that remains here 'till then
are only memories, and rumors of war.

So if you want to be a writer here,
you only need to know where to get the shirt.
As for material, you just have to sift it,
'cause it never was nothing but dirt.
Fallen Empire, causes notwithstanding,
the reason for your existence is beyond understanding.
Like nightfall before noon with its shadows unending,
a horse only keeps on running
if he knows where he's heading.

What we take as our lifetimes,
filled as they are with strife,
are really massive exercises in futility
conducted in the absence of light.

The Fallen Empire is the place where
this has all come to pass.
It's no use to replay the litany
of eternal harass.

Shame and disgrace
in a land without honor,
remembrance is the cruelest,
it lays waste to April.

The morning is for recreation,
the evening is for contemplation,
every day is an exercise in futility
that defies explanation.

Fallen Empire, with your beard like moss,
Fallen Empire, with your legs like dross,
stand down, for it's your last season,
and your claims, like your works, are dust.

In the Fallen Empire they say we must obey
or something bad will happen.
When all of it's districts are laid to waste,
perhaps then doors will begin to be opened.

In the Fallen Empire the reins
are in the hands of the rider,
and the cry is death to all those
who aren't insiders.

Fallen Empire, your gods are dust and ash.
All you do is pose questions that no one dares ask.
However did things get this way,
how long could it possibly last?

Fallen Empire, beyond memory,
there's no recompense for your excess.
Your destruction is already complete,
but who will clean up the mess?

Fallen Empire, without meaning,
without beginning or end,
tell me why you even existed,
but first tell me when.

Is there no way that humanity can reach higher
than the empty cubicles of the fallen empire?
Is that all there is, does life have no meaning,
or is it because the universe is still dreaming?

It is beauty that poisons your hearts
in the Fallen Empire, so that it is only
oblivion that awaits you. Love is not gone,
it never was nor ever could it be, here.

In your hearts you know it's true what I say!
Fallen Empire, gone forever and today,
so that no one will remember
why you ever were, fallen empire.

How was the morning, then,
and how is the evening now
in the Fallen Empire?
As holy as the moss on a gravestone.

Gone, like the seabirds of summer
on the first day of winter;
gone like the song in my heart
when the seasons turn.

Gone like the springtime of the heart,
gone with the forests that burn,
alone like the wind in the rigging,
trying in vain to find its way home.

The Fallen Empire is the scourge
of humanity's learning curve,
because they tell you how and what to believe
so you'll forget all that matters is love.

If you change questions into answers,
and leave the dead to pile up and rot,
the foremost thing you will remember,
is everything you have forgot.

We need to take back the day
from all the shame and disgrace,
so humanity may rise up again,
now that the empire has fallen.

You can curse God and die,
and forget there are birds in the sky
alongside the devils that fly
over the fallen empire.

This feudal empire is one with eternal night,
and until it is truly fallen,
we all dwell in the absence of light.
The system of oppression makes it seem right.

Like a walking cutlass,
I cut right, left and center,
and like a true story,
I defy to be censored.

In exile for a lifetime because of their crimes,
I hold only one ambition:
to be a dancer at the end of time.
They'll all be in their graves by then.

So pencil me in for one last dance,
remember that choice leaves no recompense,
and remember also that time marches on,
and doesn't give quarter or love where there's none.

Every day is Emancipation Day
if you survive in the Fallen Empire.
Why resort to force and beat a dead horse
when diligence is all that's required.

Sitting, for now, on the dung heap of history,
forever doesn't seem like an option.
But at the end of time there'll be no reason
to be kind, and everything will surely be forgotten.

Cover me with ashes, cover me with hope,
while I run for another cover
where I can pretend again to cope
until things finally begin to turn over.

Fallen Empire, like the seasons,
you run in place 'till you fall.
Gone are the sweet long days of summer,
now they taste only of ashes, bitter as gall.

I'm leaving here in the morning,
I can't say when I'll be back again.
I'm goin' where the grocery stores
will still give me a plastic bag.

Because the higher the monkey climb,
the further he ass does show,
people will always ask too many questions,
but it's the answer they don't wish to know.

Tell me another Anansi story,
one that nobody can even recall,
about the horse that pulled the cart,
and tore it apart, 'cause the field wasn't level at all.

Here, in the Fallen Empire, we are all suspect.
Are we moral and righteous enough
that we can be expected to obey the oppressor?
Or be true to ourselves and wait for the lash to fall.

Have we found our home country at long last?
Are the stripes we all wear proof enough
of our humanity, are they the oppressor's
last gasp? Home is the heartache, perchance.

The clock and the calendar for once both agree:
the flags are at half staff all over this quiet country,
for the empire is indeed fallen, and will
forever remain, until even the dust is dust.

They say God never gives you more than you can bear,
but oppression will tax and attack you
'till the time comes when it's not quite dark yet,
in the Fallen Empire, but it's surely gettin' there.

Freedom is the only word left
to lose when all else is lost.
A penny is only worth a penny,
and only then in your thoughts.

It comes with a price, yes, a terrible cost,
for the empire has fallen and everything is lost.
Wait for the new morning, cry for a new day,
stand up and be reckoned, before it all goes away.
Can you remember the songs that were sung?
Were they the reason for what has been done?
How high climbs the monkey, how high flies the bird,
they ass will show further an you speak the word.

To be a poet in exile and to want
to be there for the dance at the end of time,
how can this ever be reconciled
with a life lived in the shadow of crime?

To exist without a face, to never have a name,
to stand in the shadows and remain there
forever, or will release finally come
once the empire has fallen?

Ashes are ashes, and dust is still dust.
When the megrims are upon you,
the fantods must be close.
Babylon must fall for the truth to appear.

Like a light in the night,
like shelter from the storm,
it's like the illusion of justice
in a world gone so wrong.

Why did I write this poem,
to indict your complacency,
or was there a reason
far beyond simple understanding?

It is not the hand of Mercy
that they call the mojo hand,
it is the curse of an ancient monkey
that once wanted to be a man.

How can the fall come
with hate and greed in our hearts,
in a world where the wicked prosper
and babies are sold for spare parts?

We walk upon the road that they paved with our bones
and march to the snare drum of fate,
until we rise up in a human race insurrection,
and claim back our love from their hate.

If you try to spell extinction,
and it comes out batalee,
then you know what I've been saying about
the difference between rakon and greed.

So charge the gates of Hell
and run 'way from Hospital,
for age is just a number
that doesn't mean anything at all.

The batalee comes so slowly,
and he comes from a place so far,
but he comes straight a sand
following a turtle star.

So when the Empire was mighty,
batalee fed the people.
But now his day is done
and the turtle star is stardust.

* * * *

You can see what I'm talking about if you know that the batalee is
a sea turtle, the leatherback, the biggest and oldest of the sea turtles.
It has gone extinct in some places because of sustained predation
until it's numbers were reduced below the minimum needed for self
propagation. This is a metaphor for our times because the greatest
things with the longest prehistoric lineage have often been sacrificed
for a few more generations of human survival. Next on the list, after
the living fossils, are fossil fuels. When these are done, as they surely
will be, a worldwide environmental and economic collapse will ensue,
allowing the lowest common denominator to prevail, precipitating
war to extinction. To prevent this, if it is at all possible, we must seek
and somehow find harmony with our ravaged planet. To my mind,
this is your only sensible recourse. For me, my only option, though
personally unobtainable due to my lack of pitch, is to go out singing.
For those who do not care: c'est le guerre.

For although this truth is never spoken,
love is war in the Fallen Empire.
For each their own choice,
be it weapon or desire.

The existence of the Fallen Empire
has been written since time began,
and the bread of sorrow has been baked
and served solely for the ruination of mankind.

I met my brethren on the street
and I told them where they had their feet.
I said, "We can lime here, but this lime have no juice."
They talked about small thing, then, that had no earthly use.

Gone again, and yet again,
unto an evening without end.
The purposelessness of existence
must pall before life begins.

How can you say that it all means something,
after all, when questions go unanswered
by the Queen of the Mall, and the reason for
her existence makes our flesh crawl?

Gone already, before you got started,
gone already down a path only half hearted,
come if you may, yes come if you will
and dwell for awhile in a house on the hill.

In the Fallen Empire, the lickerish take first bite,
and the sweetness of life then dies in their mouth.
Rage, rage, against the dying of the light,
Rhygin go rage still, after it goes out.

People always want to talk about something,
but they don't know what to say.
So they think by workin' Obeah
they go salvage themselves half a day.

When the war is inside you,
it has to be fought in the heart,
There can never be a winner,
and loss will tear you apart.

Religion is the poison in the soul of mankind,
but the heart has it's seasons that are as old as time.
If you search for freedom in a world full of lies,
truth is the only answer, but it's impossible to find.

I have apples like tears, and the tears fall like rain,
I can't begin to tell you, the words sound so insane,
it all belongs in the fire, eternity's claim,
but the hand that planted them remains in the Fallen Empire.

Dust is like ashes, and ashes are like dust.
See beyond what they cover and do what you must.
Then, only then, will the rain come down
on this entire massive exercise in futility.

They call it, sometimes, history,
also sometimes the history of humanity,
but I say it's the history of oppression,
a litany of what has gone wrong since civilization began.

How have you seen the fallen empire?
Was it through the glass of "where I belong"?
Or was it intellectual bereavement
that made you unable to remember the song?

I know someone once must have warned you,
and I know it turned out this way,
but if you can't come to some higher understanding,
then I'm left without anything to say.

So the ending is thus, and now it has come,
and it's everything it appears to be,
I have given my heart and my soul
for nothing, in this lonesome country.

Now oblivion awaits you,
it's the final frontier,
and in your wake there are only
remembrance, and rumors of war.

Fallen Empire, spiritual vampire,
nothing from you is any use.
Rhygin's day is done, but again he will come,
and not in sheep's clothing next time.

Eternal City

In the world as it is,
which had no beginning in this,
and no reason to answer or call;
no, there's no answer here at all;
yet something, there is, and it's not a near miss,
for Babylon has yet to fall.
And so the projections
for humanity's resurrection
are in no way accurate, at all.

In the eternal wasteland of Babylon exists the concept of acquiescence. Complacency and industry for eternity is the litany of progress in modern thought. We have to change the way we appear to ourselves: neither modern, retroactive, recidivist nor hegemonist, otherwise we will never find freedom at all.

It is not wise to tell a politician
that he pulls the cart of oppression,
for he doesn't realize he's a horse, after all.
The Empire has been fallen since it's inception,
and has yet to hear its name call.

Forward is ever and backward is never,
I hope I'll not have to repeat.
You need to find a new road,
one that leads the way home for your feet.

Probably, it would be more correct to call it the *Internal City*, since it's only Babylon in your mind. It's the city state that defines us, to keep our minds on our purse so God can reimburse us for our meaningless existence. It is the land of oppression, and everyone likes that just fine, and nobody complains all the time.

What else is there in life
but the fulfillment of desire,
or the absence thereof
that feeds the flames higher?

Tell me this city is eternal,
and I will show you the lie
upon which it was founded.
Cry wolf on your steppes,
like they have you surrounded.

After awhile there, you know
that life is a gamble,
and that what you make there
isn't the only answer.

Other Writings

Wait for the West Wind

Wait for the West Wind
to come and fill your sails.
Wait for a hot day
to start out on the trail.
Remember me in a bird's song,
and in the ring around the sun.
Remember me when the work is finished,
remember me when the day is done.

I'll be gone for a long time,
and you'll likely not see how it ends.
Summer's long days are ending,
and I'll not see the spring again.
Hear me, my children,
I give you my heart and my soul.
And though love pretends to be never ending,
it's the end of life that's so cold.

———————————

Who Am I

(chorus)

Who am I,
to stand and wonder,
to wait,
while the wheels of fate
slowly grind my life away?
Who am I?

There were some things
that I loved one time,
but the dreams are gone
I thought were mine,
and the hidden tears,
that once did fall,
now burn inside
at the thought of all;
the years of waste,
the years of crime,
the passions of a heart so blind,
to think that,
but even, still,
as I stand exposed
the feelings are felt,
and I cry into
the echo of my loneliness.

(chorus)

What a nothing
I've made of life,
the empty words,
the coward's plight,
to be pushed and passed
from hand to hand,
never daring to speak,
never daring to stand.
And the emptiness
of my family's eyes
reminds me over and over of lies,
and promises, and deeds undone,
and now again I want to run,
but now, there is
nowhere to run to.
(chorus)

And now, my friend,
we meet again,
and we shall see
which one will bend
under the strain
of death's golden eyes,
which one of us
shall win the prize,
to live and
which one will die.
'Tis I, my friend,
yes, 'tis I.
To kill to live,
again and again,
to clutch the throat
of sweet revenge,
for life is here only
for the taking.

Ted Torgersen

Who am I

to stand and wonder,

to wait,

while the wheels of fate

slowly grind my life away?

Who am I?

Who am I?

The Ivory Towers of Babylon

In the anti-intellectual climate of today we see that the "dumbing down" of higher education is at once the lapdog of the post-industrial feudalistic hegemony and the running dog of bourgeois complacency, and although this is rather obvious, what is not so apparent, at least on the surface, is that it is also the bugbear of the all but invisible intelligentsia, which has disappeared before everyone's eyes but its own to the point where not only can no one see it, it can scarcely even see itself. The diploma mills compete to turn out, not ranks of scholars or thinkers, but the eager drudges that are the mainstay of bureaucracies everywhere, assuring that society remains unthreatened by new ideas and that the long-legged wolf of consumerism runs unchecked as the lead dog in the world-wide Iditarod of capitalist oppression. Perhaps serious intellectuals should consider adopting The Negro National Anthem* as their own and rally against the intramural complacency that has plagued our universities and colleges for decades. At least the tenured ones need not fear reprisals for insubordination other than the revocation of those human rights that they have already abdicated, consigning intellectuals to the role of invisible strangers, and denying that adherence to outspoken intelligent views was a human right to begin with.

Though it seems ludicrous in retrospect, Maoist rhetoric, while in itself fiercely anti-intellectual and of the basest knee-jerk simplicity, helps apply a grimly humorous perspective to the plight of the world's intellectual community, if, in any real sense, it can be said to still possess one. The two great social philosophies, Laissez-Faire Capitalism and Stalinist-Maoist Communism, have supplanted religion in modern times, and while the conflict raged, served to mitigate each the deleterious effects of the other on the hapless population of the world. During this time intellectual pursuits and scholarship were suppressed to maintain a unified ideological front, equally on both sides, while maintaining the fiction that it was only a temporary measure. Now that worldwide consumerism is the sole ideology, and The Job has displaced The God as the ideal, there is nothing left to hold back the tide of rootlessness and destruction as it sweeps through traditional cultures and attacks the natural world, all in the name of progress. Thus educational institutions turn out workers rather than thinkers and the goal is a better Job thus more buying power hence more consumerism ad infinitum ad nauseum. Only the mind itself remains unconquered, and by keeping the pursuit of truth at bay with promises of spare parts and money, intellectualism is fast becoming an historical curiosity, for the agenda of oppression can only be opposed by truth, just as darkness can only be conquered by light. We must turn away, like the Garveyites of old, from empty promises, and learn to rely on ourselves alone for the ideas that sustain our mental lives, for race is no longer an issue when our very humanity is at stake.

We, the current generation of potential scholars, must shake off the lethargy that comes with a surfeit of entertainment and create our own intellectual renaissance. It is long overdue, and we can no longer be content with inspiration from past great thinkers like Henry David Thoreau in his Walden wilderness, or Marcus Garvey gleefully exiled to Ghana, or even V. S. Naipaul, returned, at last, to Trinidad. Learning and the pursuit of knowledge is not a football match between the red team and the blue team, but must be recognized as a struggle with the mechanics of metaphysics, lest our own ivy clad towers of refuge, like castles made of sand, crumble into a sea of mediocrity. A new intelligentsia must be cut out of whole cloth, or like Pallas Athena spring full blown from the minds of our generation. We must create for ourselves what no one will create for us.

*We Shall Overcome

The Invisible Stranger

Who am I now,
and what was I before
in that uncertain country
that I couldn't take, anymore?
Inaction has consequences too:
if I see nothing, say nothing,
hear nothing, fait rien,
I am nothing, and no one can see me,
nor where I am not,
nor what I'm not doing.

If a leaf falls by itself in a forest,
does it make any sound?
Or does your whole play pretend castle
have to crash down around you
to get your attention?
Can I man walk naked down Main Street,
lighting invisible bonfires
that smell faintly
like the funeral pyre
of lost love?

Dance away, and no one will see you,
slip away and no one will know
you were ever there.
Make a little pile of leaves and feathers
to show that nobody cares.
Burn down Babylon
with the fire of truth
and forget that you ever had a name.

The New Nothing

The newer the nothingness,
the more it unfolds that
it's not that it's newer,
it just isn't old.
It's so hard to figure
and can't be bought or sold,
or used to make the climate more temperate,
or a soldier more bold;
or to remember anything
nor even to forget,
and month after month
it's a source of regret.

There was always
something called nothing,
and even before that,
there was nothing called something,
it hadn't been invented yet.
More like a whistle
than the wind on a pond,
more like the morning
than the day later on;
it meets the road in the middle
'cause it just can't go on
in a world that's gone to China.

———

Lost Soldier, Carry the Load

Happy are the soldiers
now that the battle is won.
Yes, happy because
they had the good sense to run.
Happier still are the valiant,
those who did what they must;
their race is now run,
their faces to the dust.

Long ago, when war was new,
people spoke of honor,
and fought the whole day through.
Now the world is older,
and there's less and less to say;
war is just a business,
and the dead don't draw pay.

When last was harmony
the song in mankind's heart?
Dig the Earth and draw the water
from where they buried what was lost.
If it should rise back up,
now that love is gone,
all the happy soldiers could live
to sing a devastation song.

————————

Ted Torgersen

Turtles All the Way Down*

He squeaked through that one
by a turtle hair,
which is another way of saying
he had nothing to spare,
'cause there ain't no such thing,
there's no room there,
and because turtles don't care,
that's why they live so long.

Love brings you into this life
and then it gives you the lie,
so, in the end it's the things you care about
that make you suffer before you die.
That's why turtles live the longest,
and their meat tastes so sweet,
especially those that live in the sea
and have flippers instead of feet.

Infinity is forever,
but it isn't the turtles' fault
that we're left here to wonder why,
and turtles cry tears of salt.

* From *Thunder of Time* by James E David.

Once on a journey, a philosopher encountered an old man and asked the old man to describe the world's place in the universe. "That's easy," the old man said, "the world is a great ball resting on the back of a giant turtle." "But what is the turtle standing on?" the philosopher asked. "Another, larger turtle," the old man replied. "And what is this turtle standing on?" asked the philosopher. "You can't trick me," the old man shot back. "It's turtles all the way down."

The Terror of the Tadpole

It's like the plight of nature
in the modern world,
like the fate of the tadpole,
swimming in a toilet bowl.
Even if, when you flush it,
the water is still clean,
he still goin' someplace else,
and will never again be see.

But what of our tadpole, now,
who'll never be a frog?
How far will he make it
if the drains aren't clogged?
To die all alone in the salt of the sea,
or drown in a septic tank,
and still be close to me;
if he lies, forgotten,
on some nameless shore,
then all that's left of his story
are remembrances,
and rumors of war.

———————

Home Is the Hero

Home is the hero,
don't you worry no more.
The journey lies behind him,
even the marks of high water
that remain on the signs
by the side of the road
where he passed
are only reminders
of his struggle to cross Acheron.
But before he did,
not only had she sealed up the book
wherein he wrote all wrongs,
he was stuck in the middle of nowhere,
and they had already closed the door.
But he knew it was just the door
to another place that had been nailed shut,
and he had no business goin' there,
but it didn't haunt him like it did before,
'cause Heaven is filled up with strangers
that he didn't want to meet,
and people from the past
that he didn't even know anymore.

The floodwaters had receded,
and the way was now clear,
horizon to horizon,
without meaning,
without fear.
Nobless Oblige had paid the toll
and left the rent in arrears,
so the road was wide open,
the way was all clear.
There were many rivers to cross
on the way there,
but when he turned away
only one remained.
He could see the gates
he had so foolishly charged,
armed with the fires of youth
and a pail of water,
and that he optimistically once
had painted a gleaming black,
where they awaited him
on that farther shore.

The paint was peeling now,
and there were scorch marks
from all the wars, I guess.
Even the hinges had rusted,
and one gate hung crooked,
looks like nobody comes here, anymore.
Even the ferryman had left
and taken a job ashore,
so he took his time
and crossed that final river
on a raft that he made, himself,
out of sticks.

———————

Ted Torgersen

A Garden At Death's Door

Hers* were always flowers,
but a condemned man
deserves a hearty meal,
so I planted a vegetable garden
right in front of death's door.
It go be a while before it bear.

The potatoes alone
would take more than two months.
A few carrots wouldn't be bad,
and a cabbage or two would work.
A short hedge of peas,
a tomato plant or two,
and a few other things
without which you can't do.

Learn to live alone,
and dying is easy,
or so some people believe.
Dying is like crying;
if you can't do one
then you can't do the other.
First you must cry,
then you can die,
you go eat your last meal
bye and bye.

*For Emily Dickenson, a great poet who lived a loveless, reclusive
life and whose works were only published and widely acclaimed after
her death. I don't know if I stole the title for this or not, but I thought
of her and this is by way of tribute.

All of my devils
are standing here in line,
there's nothing I can do about it,
so I'll just take my time.
Remembering what was
is easier than being here now,
and even easier than that
is to forever forget how.

Like the food in a food ad,
or a bakery without an oven,
cast aside for no reason,
I'm left with a small portion,
and I don't have enough strength
to dig my own grave,
or even write my own epitaph.

———————

West Indies in Transition:
Bay to Guest House

Long time me usta be deh a bay, but me deh deh a guest house now. Place changeup an' rough sea come an' wash way the beach a bay so no seine can't come shore again an' de place get modern. A' we usta cook a fireside, make tea on pitchoil stove, carry bucket a water from the pipe. We had candle and pitchoil lamp for light and latrine outside. That was how thing was a bay. Where me deh now get sink wit' pipe inside, hot water, all as that, bathroom, shower, fridge, gas stove, current and all, even tv. Funny how as t'ing get bigger, money get smaller, what was big money long time a small change now. Still, ah we so a movin' up! Me deh a guest house now, no bay like long ago, and a lot has changed.

Even the way to wash wares is different. Long time we had wash pan and threw way the water a sand. Now and again we hadda rake up the yard and bury fruit skin and so forth. Now, in the guest house, the key is Vim, even se'f them no call a that again. In order to keep ants and day bats away, wit' the pipe inside, you hafta apply Vim wit' vigor! That is the key to life in the modern world of the guest house: Vim. Yeah, boy, without that you piss.

Now even cooking is different too, because you get gas stove and fridge, so it's way easier to keep thing. But the main thing is ingredients. You can get provision and coconut, like long ago, as long as you get money, and fish, if they catch, but you take sancoche, now, or oildown as some call it. Long ago it only had provision, like buck buck, fish, okra and dasheen bush, cook in coconut juice with just a tip of curry to cut the whiteness of the coconut. Now you make coconut juice with blender, no grater again, and shop have everything so you put saltfish and pigtail along with the fresh fish. But the main difference is the chicken powder. Long time we didn't have that, and long ago people would quarrel, saying how you make powder from fowl, anyway? Like you have to dry it and pound it 'till it come powder. Me se'f wonder if them bother to clean them first or just dry the fowl dem some kinda way and pound them 'till they come powder. Anyway, that does be in pot now, an' me wonder how that could be. I did gone for a long time.

How 'bout phone, now! Everybody in the whole world get phone, and here ain't no different. Long time when fish catch a bay, men usta blow conch shell an' people would know fish catch and come if they wanted to buy or to see if they could still get. Now cell phone is the thing, and sometimes engine boat does sell out they catch before they meet sand. The fishermen get new ways too, you can't scrabble fish like long ago, those who help, get. I even saw an engine boat with a long pole in the bow and a line astern with two jugs tied to it, one long and one short. Every time the breeze blow or the sea move, the jugs a fly around. Them say is to keep the big ben from nasty up the boat while it moor off. A fella tell me is no obeah he a work but a brain, a bird brain, must be. A next fella tell me he no like for leave he net a sand 'cause crab and snake does come in the night and nyam holes in the twine. Me never hear nothin' so, long time.

Another thing change up here is hoss. Long ago people usta mind hoss just like cow and so forth, sheep, goat, pig, duck, fowl, rabbit, what it have. Hoss was used as a draft animal, when people went a bush to work big garden. Nowadays people no do that much, more kitchen garden, and hoss is only for entertainment, not food or work again. All over the world is so, hoss day done. Must be 'cause all a the car it have now, it no get room for hoss again.

Well everything change up, but it still the West **Indies**, after all. You can lime out a road, take a sea bath with bush to wash the rum outta your skin, and go back and fete some more. You can eat bush meat, in season, and even taste babash here or there. All in all, the sun still shine, and rain still fall 'pon a' we. Seems like Biswas get he house long time, an now there's a place for me a guest house. However it play, I glad to be back in the land again, God 'ear.

The Garden of Love Lost

Like the sands of the beach
and the hourglass of me life,
like the love in my heart,
all is gone from me now.

When my life was half gone,
I took from Telly's garden
sweet pine, cassava,
buck buck and dasheen.
Me plant wonder of the world
and coconut tree,
and I sow sorrow seed,
to keep alive the memory
of my refuge, my home.
But then the sea came and took all.
The garden that will never bear,
it still remains there,
the something I put
by the still waters of Bay River.

If you must someday find me,
it is there I must be,
alone, forever,
between the river and the sea.

Taste the bitter coraille
mixed with the salt sea
from my palm,
in remembrance,
not of me,
but of how this came to be
in a barren garden
blasted by the sea,
and cry tears,
for the music that has stopped.

Life continues until
the suffering is enough,
beginning to end,
emptiness and loss.
And the kindness of the people here,
and the beauty of this land,
cannot help but reach me,
and make me feel so sad.

I planted that garden
to keep hope and love alive.
It always was a struggle,
there never was a reason
beyond the will to survive.
Now the salt blast
from this last rough sea
has scoured it out from this country,
and so taken the heart out of me.

The caged bird sings
only for its freedom,
never for its love,
or the wide sky above,
for it will never know them again.
The Aluminum Biscuit Dance

I had my plate full of dumplin',
I had myself a beer.
I lived my life in ignominy,
and will end my life in fear.

No one came,
and no one went,
and no one saw or cared,
and like the stranger
in the French gaol,
I said what I thought
they wanted to hear.

Why is death so frightening
to those who know it's near?
Is it because of the lives they lived,
or what they couldn't believe or feel?

Why is there only one thing
that people will willingly live without?
Why is love not the answer,
but only a cause for doubt?

You can drag the chickenheads,
on wire line,
through the eelgrass,
two at a time
and still get nothing.

It comes quickly, so seemly,
so calm and so clear,
as long as the Devil's district
is nowhere near here.
Go where you want to,
do whatever you know:
life's a mystery meat feast
that they eat in the snow.

All that is okay,
because there are
treasonous monkeys
hidden in the trees;
what nobody wants to believe is true:
that's why I told it to you.

———————

Ted Torgersen

The Bread of Sorrow

The most repeated word that you hear
in the songs of today, is "tonight".
Because of what the day brings,
the night must promise relief;
what the heart sings for
makes the spirit grieve
when it does not come.
Night and day, day and night,
bound together on the wheel of fate,
come forward, come alone, come together,
some call it a life.
But what is the bread, and who eats it?
Cassava, sourdough, wheat, white or rye,
is it not the flesh, but our very lives
that are eaten by the system
that grinds our bones to make flour?

So judgmental, so ignorant,
so shallow, so condescending,
they present, and so we listen.
More forgiving are the ones
that name them useless;
intelligence is anathema
for the alternative is destruction
in the book from which they read.
We name it The Book of Sorrows,
for we are the bread which they eat,
our sad lives a feast for the ages,
like our blood, the ink doesn't run
while their hands turn the pages.
Guiltiness is not a condition of the mind alone.
It influences thought, it's true,

but what else can it do, will you show me?
Guilt is the burden built on the back
of the oppressed which proclaims them inferior,
saying the same thing, like a loop in a string
that was left loose, again and again, forever,
or the bitterness in a biscuit
that was baked too long,
or the loneliness in a life
spent looking for love too long,
or the ending you could never remember.
Forward is the direction
that the day takes
from morning 'till evening,
light to dark to light again;
light like the sound of the skylark,
or as heavy as even like never remember.
When an eclipse occurs
it is always like something else;
why, they can't say,
no matter they can predict it.
So why can't the moon
make you hear it?
It knows something we don't,
of that there's no doubt,
it's been there for a long while,
before any child knew it
and history can't tell you why.

Better you hear what I man say,
the long dead position
that belies the tradition
of acceptance,
for there is no transition
from ancient to modern times.
No man, it was oppression then,
same as now, how it happened,

some way, some how
that leads us on to destruction.
We'll be better off dead,
like the song said,
that's what they tell us
to make us ashamed
of the fact we are even alive.
It's life itself you must dread,
you'd be better off dead,
they can't have read
the same books as I did,
or any that spoke of love.

None of those people
that never had a direction,
not any of those people
are near here, tonight,
not anywhere near here, tonight.

In the eyes of the oppressor
there is no right, no wrong.
There is only the might
that we redress here, in song.
Horizon to horizon
in the slanting light of the setting sun,
we see the field is still level
now that all the games are done.
No matter what you bet on,
with the odds in your favor,
the game is just a lie
to make us believe
in a pie in the sky.
It's really the bread of sorrow,
and though you wish for a slice,
the taste is too bitter,
better tell them "No dice."

Or say over and over
that the world ain't so nice,
or begin to tell the reason
that begins with the season
and ends in tears when you speak
over the bread that breaks you
into pieces to be cast upon the waters.

From morning's first light
to the dark of midnight,
it's time once again to slip 'way.
You hear about forgiveness,
but I wonder if it could come,
whose will must be done,
to forgive us for being ourselves,
for we are the bread of sorrow.
Sold to the lowest bidder
for the good of the country, they say,
not my country, today,
but a hidden realm
of broken dreams
and empty promises,
that forbidden dream country
whence no traveler returns,
where they bake the bread of sorrow.

———————

Scoter

Hear the spirit singin' out a warnin',
it could be the very last time,
like the wind blowin' through the wires
at the beginning of a hurricane;
they just a hummin' and a screamin'
'till they part off from the strain,
never to be heard from, again.

Meanwhile, between the river and the sea,
dozens of grey and white gulls
stand on the sand at the blocked river mouth,
as hundreds of evil, greasy looking
ducklike things spread over the calm
fresh water of the river like oil.
Their bills are white,
and every now and then one dives,
occasionally appearing to have gotten something.

So it's plain to see that they're scoters,
not ducks, and they bring nothing but bad luck,
you better take a chance and slip away.
There's other rivers to cross,
no matter what the cost,
that those diving birds want you to pay.
Yeah, man, you just better slip away.

Now, if you put all of this together,
as I know you must,
there ain't much in it to be thankful for.
Not even the dust in your hand
can level the land that you play on
as you decide to keep it or haul it about;
truth does the talkin' when you say shit out loud.
Mean Old Woman Blues

She more evil than she old,
she more wicked than she stupid,
but to my mind she's a little bit of both.
She always wants more than what it's worth.
She will ask anyone about anything she wants,
but almost never will she tell them the truth.

More times mean more questions, under the sun,
and the time to find answers has already begun,
but something still stands in the way.
You can cross rivers and oceans,
and go through all kinds a motions,
but there's nothing left, really, to say.

She's a mean old woman,
on that we all agree,
and if you want my advice
you can have it for free:
better you no business with she, yeah,
make you no bother with she.

————

A Hegemony of Hats

As many as the hats they wore,
as dense as the column
in which they marched,
as district upon district
paid them homage,
they are no more.

Teeth were gnashed,
and grim grins gritted
as baleful eyes looked on.
Remember the truth
that no one spoke,
remember the setting of the sun.

Between the mountains
and the sea
lies a road
that has never been traveled.
It leads to a fountain,
long gone dry,
in the desert
of mankind's ambitions.

———

Countrey of Dust

I will dump the smoking hot oil
unto the compost pile of America
to keep down the dust,
and its concomitant ignominy,
until life itself is beyond understanding.

Way to go, people.
Your complacency has rendered
unto Caesar all which is Caesar's,
and all the tyrants to come are in your debt.
Too bad humanity had to perish
in the meantime,
while homo sapiens lives on
in its uncounted millions.
C'est le guerre.

It's more horsed to your vessel
or more shrink to your wrap,
that's much heavier in your mind
and makes there be more hell in mine.
As you see, it's not easy,
although the answer is plain;
life is just as you see it,
so why bother to complain.

More coventry than that which covered me,
more courage than I could cry for;
more emptiness than a hollow tree,
more fruitless than an empty basket,
truth, the light I never saw.
Call again, and cry tough,
call again in the wilderness your discontent.
Rhygin, born again,
has been here and gone,
and, shoeless, danced upon all
your graves in perfect sadness.
More's to pity that no one noticed.

John Henry, Revisited

It's all in the way
you make your last stand,
just like old John Henry
with a hammer in his hand.

Most of the way,
and pret' near all the time,
when you cross the road,
you're way outta line.

So, even as ever
you see where you go
so wrong did the maker that
your roots once did sow.

That's why is life so cold, then,
like the clay in your hand,
I goin' back home now,
where I can walk like a man.

———————

Hurricane

They surely were a sorry bunch,
Americanos caught in a hurricane.
The wind blew them down to Mexico,
and now they're sorry that they came.

Life would be a lot easier
if they had just stayed at home.
The customs and the country
made them all feel so alone.

Everybody was talkin',
but they knew not what about,
the reason was the language,
of that there is no doubt.

Americanos in a dilemma,
Americanos left all alone,
wait until the storm is over
and try to find your way back home.

———————

The Harvey Gamage

I went out fishing,
the other day,
and out in the fog,
it's sometimes that way,
was a space with a sky
and white all around,
and all in a moment
when I turned around,
it seemed there was something,
I saw it was a boat.

Here come the Harvey Gamage,
right out of the fog.
There was little we could do
and nothing to say.
We could each just make way,
try as we might,
the current, you see,
had been running all night.

They were all on the back deck,
the crew, as you know;
they were laughin' and talkin'
the whole way through.
They din't do no work,
to that I can attest,
every mother's son of them
was wearin' a Panama Jack.

Shootin' seagulls off the back deck
gets old before too long;
you cry tears to the ocean,
but them old sons are gone.
They were the pride of the fleet,
you couldn't scare them away,
but the rest of us who are left
have to carry on today.

—————————

The Four Directions

Altruism

In my travels, once,
while I was crossing the road,
I really thought the devil had got me
for what he said that I owed.

I started to remember
that the night was not far off,
so I gathered up my leaflets
and began to scatter reports.

I said what I was thinking,
I talked about what I had heard;
now, looking back at it,
it all seems so absurd.

* * **

Heroism

We gonna beat the monkey,
though he creeps the whole night through.
We can't make very much of it,
despite what we wanted, too.

We gonna beat him right out of this
human thing that we do.
We keep fast to our side,
don't let nothin' get through,
and the last time we stopped them
go be remembered, for true.
Livin' here now, it's all about work.
No one will teach you how to do it,
or show you where to buy the shirt.
It's damned if you do,
but then if you don't,
it's consequences unheard of,
and perseverance only hurts.

As far as my life goes,
there's no news that is new;
I'll continue to continue
to give the devil his due;
that is, until we meet face to face.

* * * *

Realism

On the talk shows,
the host tells you what's what,
and if you ask too many questions,
they'll say, "Keep your mouth shut."
Even the dreams you can remember
are just make believe,
and everyday life gets harder and harder
'till it's time for you to leave.

The heavier your burden,
the farther there is to go,
and it seems the long years' only purpose
is to erase what you know.
Remember the beginning?
When the end was far away?
You had more questions than answers,
and each morning was a new day.
Now the sun is setting
and you have no place to go.
The night is dark and empty,
and of holiness there is none.
Try to remember, try as you might,
but nothing will stay with you
into your next life.

* * *

Schism

Exactly in between what is right
and what's wrong,
lies an imaginary boundary
that's never been mentioned in song.
The place where it starts,
and the place where it ends
is at the beginning,
where everything bends.

Bread of sorrow,
life's ambition;
open country,
life in prison;
break it open,
seal it shut;
life is a feeling
deep in your gut.

The Four Directions
are not choices.
They are the measure of the world,
yet they remain unrepentant.

———————

The Endless

The Nameless

I'm a popular man,
my friends call me every night.
But that's not my real name,
and it ain't *Tonight's the Night*.
Religion and gumbo
can be hard to tell apart;
one is more gluey than the other,
but neither comes from the heart.

Guess again, my good friend,
yes, just you guess again.
What you see is what you get,
but it's nothing you can spend.
The future and the past
are but two sides of a coin,
each representative at first
of the sides of your mind.

* * * *

The Hopeless

The helpless are hopeless
so they shun the light;
they have already lost the struggle
and so welcome the night.
The squalor of the aged
comes upon us by degrees,
like a homeward bound sailor
or a malfunctioning machine.
The shades are all lowered,
the windows shut down
against the sun of the morning,
and the soft rains to come.
Hope visits like a bird
that leaves when spring comes;
by the end of the summer
there'll be nobody home.

* * * *

The Rootless

The homeless are in Heaven,
that's why they have no homes.
The world is but their pasture
where they live out lives alone.
People wonder why they don't
put down roots like a tree.
They can't see that the reasons
are like the fish in the sea.

Wind makes the waves and current,
the moon makes the tides;
the sojourner passes through places
but nowhere does he abide.
The reasons are many,
both to stay or to go;
the answer is in your question,
but it's nothing you could know.

* * **

The Thoughtless

The mindless are loveless
and careless and cold,
they march in lockstep,
both the young and the old.
Their minds empty as a pocket,
their gaze as wide as the sky,
their eyes are on the horizon,
and they never ask why.

The thinkers are all quiet,
do not disturb.
They know about the procession,
but they dastn't say a word.
Forward is backward,
from beginning to end,
if life had a meaning
the story could be told.

———————

Conclusion: After the Fall

The purpose of a journey is the experience, not the destination, thus the spirit's wanderings can be long indeed, with only to spread joy for a motive, not to arrive anywhere. Babylon looks like a place to leave the road, but it's a dead end. Once there, oppression traps the spirit, and the journey continues without the traveler, for the road is endless.

When the mind works a little, one thinks. When it works a lot, one wonders. But if you try to remember why you will fail. Chief Seattle said it best, but my version is this: "I will write no more, forever."

December 2014

Addendum

Author's Note

These few poems and songs didn't make the first edition due to time constraints and other random factors. I am including them in the second edition. The songs were written long ago, the first four when I was in my teens. *Nothing Sweeter Than You* was written in 1984, when I was thirty five, in Tobago, at the same time as *Where Are You Been Gone*, a tribute to the late V. S. Naipaul. The poem *Why Try* was written in 2013 and was left out so that the table of contents of *Fallen Empire and Other Writings* could fit on one page.

Again, I have no provenance for these old songs, but my quest for truth and artistic integrity bid me include them now. *The Wreck of the Edmund Fitzgerald* commemorates a real maritime disaster on the Great Lakes in the 1970s. It was a regional hit in the New England maritime community, and is my only attempt at writing a ballad. *Carefree Highway* was the swan song of that period of my life.

Respectfully submitted,

November 2019

Ted Torgersen

Follow

Let the river rock you like a cradle,
climb to the treetops, child, if you're able,
let your hands tie a knot across the table.
Come, and touch the things you cannot feel,
and close your fingertips
and fly where I can't hold you,
let the sun rain fall
and let the dewy clouds enfold you,
and maybe you can sing to me
the words that I just told you.
If all the things you feel ain't what they seem,
then don't mind me, 'cause
I ain't nothin' but a dream.

The mockingbird sings each different song.
Each song has wings, they won't stay long.
To those who hear, think he's doing wrong,
while the church bell tolls its one note song,
and the school bell is tinkling to the throng.
Come here where your ears cannot hear,
and close your ears, child,
and listen to what I'll tell you.
Follow in the darkest night
the sounds that may impel you,
and the song that I'm singing
may disturb or serve to quell you.
If all the sounds you hear ain't what they seem,
then don't mind me, 'cause
I ain't nothin' but a dream.

The rising smell of fresh cut grass,
smothered cities choke and yell with fuming gas.
I hold some grapes up to the sun,
and their flavor breaks upon my tongue.
With eager tongues we taste our strife,
and fill our lungs with seeds of life.
Come taste and smell the waters of our time,
and close your lips, child, so softly I might kiss you,
let your flower perfume mount
and let the wind caress you.
As I walk on through the garden,
I am hoping I don't miss you.
If all the things you taste ain't what they seem,
then don't mind me, 'cause
I ain't nothin' but a dream.

The sun and moon both arise,
and we'll see them soon through days of night.
But now, silver leaves or mirrors bring delight,
and the color of your eyes are firey bright,
while darkness blinds the skies with all its light.
Come see where your eyes cannot see,
and close your eyes, child,
and look at what I'll show you,
let your mind go reeling out,
and let the breezes blow you,
and maybe when we meet, suddenly I will know you.
If all the things you see ain't what they seem,
then don't mind me, 'cause
I ain't nothin' but a dream.

And you can follow,
and you can follow,
follow...

Handsome Johnny

Hey, looky yonder, tell me what you see,
marchin' to the fields of Concord?
Looks like Handsome Johnny
with a musket in his hand,
marching to the Concord War.
Hey, marching to the Concord War.

Hey, looky yonder, tell me what you see,
marchin' to the fields of Gettysburg?
Looks like Handsome Johnny
with a flintlock in his hand,
marching to the Gettysburg War.
Hey, marching to the Gettysburg War.

Chorus

And it's a long hard road,
it's a long hard road,
it's a long hard road,
hey, before we'll be free.

Hey, looky yonder, tell me what you see,
marchin' to the fields of Dunkirk?
Looks like Handsome Johnny
with a carbine in his hand,
marching to the Dunkirk War.
Hey, marching to the Dunkirk War.

Hey, looky yonder, tell me what you see,
marchin' to the fields of Korea?
Looks like Handsome Johnny with an M1 in his hand,
marching to the Korean War.
Hey, marching to the Korean War.

Chorus

Hey, looky yonder, tell me what you see,
marchin' to the fields of Vietnam?
Looks like Handsome Johnny with an M15,
marching to the Vietnam War.
Hey, marching to the Vietnam War.

Hey, looky yonder, tell me what you see,
marching to the fields of Birmingham?
Looks like Handsome Johnny
with his hand rolled in a fist,
marching to the Birmingham War.
Hey, marching to the Birmingham War.

Hey, what's the use of singing this song,
some of you are not even listening.
Tell me what it is we've got to do,
wait for our fields to start glistening?
Wait for the bullets to start whistling?
Here comes a hydrogen bomb,
and here comes a guided missile.
Here comes a hydrogen bomb,
I can almost hear it whistle,
I can almost here it whistle.

High Flyin' Bird

There's a high flying bird,
flying way up in the sky.
And I wonder if she looks down
as she goes on by,
when she's flying so free and easy
in the sky.

(Chorus)

Lord, look at me,
I'm rooted like a tree.
Got those sit down, can't cry,
oh, Lord, I'm gonna die blues.

Now, the sun, it comes up
and it lights up the day,
and when he gets tired, Lord,
and goes on down his way,
to the East and to the West,
he meets God every day.

(Chorus)

Now I had a woman, Lord,
she lived down by the mine.
She ain't never seen the sun,
oh, Lord, never stopped trying.
Then one day my woman up and died.
Lord, she up and died, now.
Oh, Lord, she up and died.
Hey, she wanted to fly,
and the only way to fly
is die, die, die.
Well, there's a high flying bird,
flying way up in the sky,
and I wonder if she looks down
as she goes on by.
Well, she's flying so free and easy,
in the sky.

(Chorus)
(Repeat chorus)

Morning, Morning

Morning, morning, feel so lonesome in the morning;
morning, morning, morning brings me grief.
Sunshine, sunshine, sunshine laughs upon my face,
and the secret of the shining
puts me in my running place.

Evening, evening, feel so lonesome in the evening;
evening, evening, evening brings me grief.
Moonshine, moonshine,
moonshine dots the hills with grace,
and the glory of the shining
seems to break my simple pace.

Night time, night time,
feel so lonesome in the night time,
night time, night time, does not bring me to relief.
Starshine, starshine, chills the moon upon my cheek,
starshine, starshine, darling kiss me as I weep.

The Wreck of the Edmund Fitzgerald

The legend lives on, from the Chippewa on down,
of the big lake they call Gitche Gumee.
The lake, it is said, never gives up her dead
when the skies of November turn gloomy.
With a load of iron ore,
twenty six thousand tons more
than the Edmund Fitzgerald weighed empty,
that good ship and true was a bone to be chewed
when the gales of November came early.

The ship was the pride of the American side,
coming back from some mill in Wisconsin.
As the big freighters go, it was bigger than most,
with a crew and good captain well seasoned.
Concluding some terms with a couple of steel firms,
when they left fully loaded for Cleveland,
then later that night, when the ship's bell rang,
could it be the North wind they'd been feelin'?

The wind in the wires made a tattle tale sound,
when the wave broke over the railing.
And every man knew, as the captain did too,
'twas the witch of November come stealin'.
The dawn came late and the breakfast had to wait
when the gales of November came slashin'.
When afternoon came, it was freezing rain
in the face of a hurricane West wind.

When suppertime came the old cook came on deck,
sayin' "Fellas, it's too rough to feed ya."
At seven pm a main hatchway caved in.

323

He said, "Fellas, it's been good to know ya."
The captain wired in he had water comin' in,
and the good ship and crew was in peril.
And later that night, when his lights went out of sight,
came the wreck of the Edmund Fitzgerald.

Does anyone know where the love of God goes
when the waves turn the minutes to hours?
The searchers all say they'd have made Whitefish Bay
if they'd put fifteen more miles behind her.
They might have split up,
or they might have capsized,
they may have broke deep and took water.
And all that remains is the faces and the name
of the wives and the sons and the daughters.

Lake Huron rolls, Superior sings,
in the rooms of her ice-water mansions.
Old Michigan steams like a young man's dreams,
the islands and bays are for sportsmen.
And farther below, Lake Ontario
takes in what Lake Eerie can send her.
And the iron boats go, as the mariners all know,
with the gales of November remembered.

In a musty old hall in Detroit they prayed,
in the Maritime Sailors' Cathedral.
The church bell chimed 'till it rang twenty-nine times
for each man on the Edmund Fitzgerald.
The legend lives on, from the Chippewa on down,
of the big lake they call Gitche Gumee.
Superior, they said, never gives up her dead
when the gales of November come early.

Why Try

Fear is the mind killer,
fear is the empty basket
at the end of the day.
Fear is the track
of a nameless insect
that cuts across
your footprint in the sand
just after you pass.
Fear is the letter that begins
"I hope you'll understand…"
even though it doesn't matter,
either way.

Those that know that night is near
dwell in endless caves of fear,
and the end matters only to itself.
But I was the end,
back at the beginning,
so, now, it also matters to me.

Ted Torgersen

Sloop John B

We come on the sloop John B,
my grandfather and me,
around Nassau Town we did roam.
Drinkin' all night,
got into a fight,
well I feel so broke up,
I wanna go home.

(Chorus)

So, hoist up the John B sail,
see how the mainsail sets,
call for the captain, ashore,
let me go home,
let me go home,
I wanna go home, yeah, yeah.
Well I feel so broke up,
I wanna go home.

The first mate he got drunk,
broke in the captain's trunk,
the constable had to come
and take him away.
Sherriff John Stone,
why don't you leave me alone, yeah, yeah.
Well I feel so broke up,
I wanna go home.

(Chorus)

The poor cook, he caught the fit,
threw away all my grits,
and then he took
and he ate up all of my corn.
Let me go home.
Why don't they let me go home?
This is the worst trip
I've ever been on.

(Chorus)

Nothing Sweeter Than You

Darlin', you're sweet, sweet, sweet, sweet,
there is nothing sweeter than you.
Darlin' you're sweet, sweet, sweet, sweet,
there is nothing sweeter than you.

Oh gal, gal, gal, you're sweet, sweet.
Oh gal, gal, gal, you're sweet, sweet.

A hot coocoo,
a hot oildown,
a hot callaloo,
ackee, saltfish and buns,
but, there is nothing sweeter than you, my darling,
(darlin' you're sweet).
There is nothing sweeter than you, my love,
(darlin' you're sweet).
There is nothing sweeter than you, my darling,
(darlin' you're sweet).
There is nothing sweeter than you, my love.

Rosey, (you sweeter than that),
conkie, (you sweeter than that),
coffee, (you sweeter than that),
sweetie, (you sweeter than that),
but, there is nothing sweeter than you, my darling,
(darlin' you're sweet)
there is nothing sweeter than you, my love.

A hot breadfruit,
a hot roast corn,
a hot corn soup,
sucking cane since I born,
but there is nothing sweeter than you, my darling,
(darlin' you're sweet).
There is nothing sweeter than you, my love,
(darlin' you're sweet).
There is nothing sweeter than you, my darling,
(darlin' you're sweet)
there is nothing sweeter than you, my love.

Nut cake, (you sweeter than that)
roast fish, (you sweeter than that)
pork skin, (you sweeter than that)
punkin, (you sweeter than that).

Oh gal, gal, gal, you're sweet, sweet.
Oh gal, gal, gal, you're sweet, sweet.
Oh gal, gal, gal, you're sweet, sweet.
Oh gal, gal, gal, you're sweet, sweet.
Darlin' you sweet, sweet sweet, sweet,
there is nothing sweeter than you.
Darlin' you sweet, sweet, sweet, sweet,
there is nothing sweeter than you.

A hot pork chop,
a hot sea egg soup,
a hot pepper pot,
a hot rice and stew,
but there is nothing sweeter than you, my darling,
(darlin' you're sweet)
there is nothing sweeter than you, my love.
(darlin' you're sweet)
There is nothing sweeter than you, my darling,
(darlin' you're sweet)
there is nothing sweeter than you, my love.

Hot coconut bread,
pudding and souse,
for years I been fed
food from my mother house,
but there is nothing sweeter than you, my darling,
(darlin' you're sweet).
There is nothing sweeter than you, my love.
(darlin' you're sweet)
There is nothing sweeter than you, my darling,
(darlin' you're sweet)
there is nothing sweeter than you, my love.

Mauby, (you're sweeter than that)
honey, (you're sweeter than that)
egg and cheese, (you're sweeter than that)
black figs. (you're sweeter than that)

There is nothing sweeter than you, my darling, (darlin' you sweet).
There is nothing sweeter than you, my love.

Dasheen, (you're sweeter than that)
ice cream, (you're sweeter than that)
sickel fig, (you're sweeter than that)
nut cake, (you're sweeter than that)
doubles, (you're sweeter than that)
sugar apples, (you're sweeter than that)
chocolate, (you're sweeter than that)
banana bake, (you're sweeter than that)

pone,
pork bone,
chicken,
fried plantain.

Oh gal, gal, gal, you sweet, sweet,
oh gal, gal, gal, you sweet, sweet,
oh gal, gal, gal, you sweet, sweet,
oh gal, gal, gal, you sweet, sweet.

Carefree Highway

Pickin' up the pieces
of my sweet, shattered dreams,
I wonder how
the old folks are tonight.

Her name was Anne,
and I'll be damned
if I recall her face.
She left me not knowin'
what to do.

(first chorus)

Carefree highway,
lets me slip away on you.
Carefree highway,
you've seen better days,
the morning after blues,
from my head
down to my shoes.
Carefree highway,
lets me slip away,
slip away on you.

Turnin' back the pages
to the times I loved best,
I wonder if she'll
ever do the same.
Now the thing that I call livin'
is just bein' satisfied,
knowin' I got no one
left to blame.

(second chorus)

Carefree highway,
got to see you,
my old friend.
Carefree highway,
you seen better days,
the morning after blues,
from my head down to my shoes.
Carefree highway
lets me slip away,
slip away on you.

Searchin through the fragments
of my dream shattered sleep,
I wonder if the years
have closed her mind.
Now, I guess it must be wanderlust,
or tryin' to get free
from the good old faithful feelin'
we once knew.

(first chorus)

(second chorus)

Sloop John B

We come on the sloop John B,
my grandfather and me,
around Nassau Town we did roam.
Drinkin' all night,
got into a fight,
well I feel so broke up,
I wanna go home.

(Chorus)

So, hoist up the John B sail,
see how the mainsail sets,
call for the captain, ashore,
let me go home,
let me go home,
I wanna go home, yeah, yeah.
Well I feel so broke up,
I wanna go home.

The first mate he got drunk,
broke in the captain's trunk,
the constable had to come
and take him away.
Sheriff John Stone,
why don't you leave me alone, yeah, yeah.
Well I feel so broke up,
I wanna go home.

(Chorus)

The poor cook, he caught the fit,
threw away all my grits,
and then he took
and he ate up all of my corn.
Let me go home.
Why don't they let me go home?
This is the worst trip
I've ever been on.

(Chorus)

Ted Torgersen
cerca 1965

www.ingramcontent.com/pod-product-compliance
Lightning Source LLC
Chambersburg PA
CBHW020433130626
46549CB00001B/110